GW00672147

I dedicate this book to my dear mother, M..,
4 November 2006 having lived to the age of 90 years, who I sadly miss.
She always looked out for me and I always looked forward to visiting her. In
2005 she came to visit me in Ripon and said.
" What a beautiful place Ripon is, if I had to live my life again then it
would be here in Ripon."
I love you Mum.

CONTENTS

ACKNOWLEDGEMENTS

In writing this guidebook at the same time as working long and arduous hours was a difficult struggle. It was enjoyable to be out walking, but the written work and recording of information required greater concentration than I had thought. I could never have finish without the encouragement of Penny Hartley, my one time neighbour, to whom I am most grateful.

To my dear friend and loved companion Margaret Ford for keeping me company along those many walks and trying out all those different cafes, teahouses and restaurants along the journeys with me.

While I discovered those that held a pessimistic view of my work, there were those close that gave me clear encouragement, my daughter Victoria and all my family members who saw my work in a rough state and commented on its potential.

A special thank you to my sister-in-law Mavis who's diligence and expertise shone through with speed and accuracy over the many spelling and grammar mistakes that I made throughout my book.

Finally I am grateful to my brother-in-law Steve Walton and my brother Bill who made up the other part of the family team to proof read my work, helping me to put my work in order.

ABOUT THE AUTHOR

Norman Finnegan enlisted into the Army in August 1980, where he joined the Royal Signals, He has served in the UK in North Yorkshire and South West Wales and overseas in Kosovo, Germany and Northern Ireland.

It was during his early years as a soldier that he discovered his great love of the outdoors in the mountains and National Parks of Great Britain.

In January 1990 he qualified as a Joint Service Mountain Expedition Leader and was moved across to work in the adventure-training world as an external leadership instructor in Harrogate. His role here was to teach navigation and leadership in a mountainous environment to recruits in the following seasons and areas: In Spring operating out of Dent, North Yorkshire. Summer the Lake District and in winter Aviemore, Scotland. He also took the opportunity to go caving, rock climbing, canoeing and winter mountaineering, with the tuition and guidance of his fellow instructors. This fantastic job went on year for four wonderful years, taking full advantage of the environment that he was employed in to go out in his spare time and enjoy the challenges of the terrain and the weather that surrounded him.

In 1992 he pursued his outdoor career by attending a Joint Service Mountain Expedition Leader (Winter) Training, and Continuation Training courses in Scotland, that entailed learning the challenges and skills in winter conditions.

Additionally he has organised and led groups on military adventure training expeditions in The Lakes District, North Yorkshire, Scotland and Wales; Overseas, in Austria, Bavaria, Canada, Germany and in the Pyrenees throughout his military career.

He now continues his adventures as a civilian bringing accurate guidance and instruction in the form of this guidebook, hopefully the first of many to come.

FOREWORD

This discovery guidebook to Ripon is written in a modern theme to point out the many interesting places worthy of a visit within the City. The Book also directs people to the numerous historic buildings located in the area and the opportunities for people to learn about many important events that occurred, including royal visits - Kings and Queens who played their part in history during their lives.

Apart from the Ripon Rowel Walk, the book includes the Sanctuary Way Walk; a walk set up around a series of sanctuary marker stones set out approximately one mile form the Cathedral. This walk relates back in time to the original sanctuary boundary hundreds of years ago.

The Ripon Rowel is a walk of approximately 50 miles that starts in the centre of Ripon and covers a large circular area taking in the tremendous scenery along the banks of the following rivers: the River Skell running west to east through Ripon, the River Ure running north to south connecting Ripon to Masham, and the River Burn just south of Masham. As well as the picturesque slightly undulating countryside, the walk cuts through many villages where you can indulge yourself by trying out the excellent food and beverages on offer, that are made locally at one of the many establishments along the way.

The walk as been split down into seven logical stages, covered in the following sections of this book that can either be walked separately, starting and returning back to Ripon each day, using transport, or continuously, that will enable you to sample and experience the local hospitality by staying over night in a different place each day.

Whatever your choice you will find the walking pleasant and easy going.

NAVIGATION

Navigation is the activity of getting from A to B, by guiding yourself along a particular route.

There are aids that will assist you: map, compass, watch, guidebook and now satellite navigation systems. You could use all of the above, though, two would be enough, and in this case, a guide book and a watch.

People each day navigate themselves around towns and along the British roads, and they do it very well; sometimes navigating without much thought because the route is well known to them. However, if you go to a new place that you have never been before, then caution is naturally applied and you travel along much more slowly, paying particular attention to what is around you. In the country on foot navigation is a little the same except for the scale and the terrain, and there are not to many sign posts to follow. Instead you have to read what is either on the map or guidebook and identify those same features to those on the ground around you and vice versa.

It is enjoyable and satisfying to get along a route that you intended to do. It is just with a little time and regular practice that you become proficient.

Distance. All distances and measurements are metric - Metres and kilometres. Each section has its own sketch maps showing a scale. 100 metres is the distance of a football pitch to help you relate to metric distance.

Speed. We have all varied levels of fitness, the standard speed to cover 1000 metres over flat level ground is 12 minutes. That means 100 metres would be covered in 1 minute 12 seconds. This rule applies to the average fit person, though a personal test would be ideal if we all have access to a football pitch. The other things that could effect your speed would be the weight that you carry on your back and what type of ground you will be covering, wet and boggy, steep or rocky ground can slow you down to the speed of a snail. Take into account ascending hills or rises on the ground. In the case of map reading that would mean crossing contour lines, for every contour line crossed extra time is required to account for the effort needed and the effect it will have on your fitness; this extra time to be added is 1 minute on to your calculated speed.

Time. By knowing the distance after measuring it on a map, and counting the contour lines that you cross, you can work out approximately how much time the days walk will take. It could be that your speed is faster or slower than 12 minutes per 1000 metres, but it is a good bench mark to practice around.

By knowing your speed you will know how far you will have travelled by the use of a stop watch; for example if you walked along a footpath for 5 minutes, then the distance would relate to 600 metres.

Map Reading. Maps are filled with information and strange symbols, and there are many types of maps. It is worth while before setting off looking at your map to familiarise yourself with all the information it holds. Within these maps there are scales that can be different. The scale on maps is the measurement of value relating to distance. It is very important to familiarise yourself with the scale on a 1000 METRES 0 KILOMETRES 1 map so that you know the distance when it is measured. You can also find out just how far a section is or all of the walk you are going to undertake. To use the map, when walking for navigation you should orientate the map in front of you, to the direction of travel. This action in many cases could mean you hold the map upside down or at any angle relating to your direction of travel and the ground features along the route; aligning the path marked on the map to the actual footpath you are walking on the ground.

Safety. Unfortunately people do get lost, or get caught out in bad weather. In the most extreme terrains people do get injured and lose their lives. Preparation for the outdoors is very important, carry suitable clothing and enough food and water, the weather conditions could change. Tell someone where you are going and when you will return.

CONDUCT IN THE COUNTRY

In the country, along the routes mentioned in this book you are required to adhere to the Country Code, which will help you along on your travels. Being practical and considerate to other walkers, farm property and farm animals will help to show that you respect the ways of the countryside, and will help to form good relationships between walkers and landowners. Being conscious and considerate can only help to protect the country side now and for future generations.

Safety.
a. Plan your journey, some of the routes in this book are over 4 hours duration, you will need to carry some basic extra clothing, food and water.
b. Check the weather forecast before you leave, and don't be afraid to cancel your day out.
c. Communications. Tell someone where you are going, and roughly what time you intend to return. Mobile telephone coverage may not be available along some of the routes
d. Know the signs and symbols used in the country.

Access.
a. Follow the footpath along the planned route.
b. Use gates and stiles along your route. Don't climb over walls and fences, this causes damage and farm animals could get out.
c. Cross fields by using the signed footpath.
d. Leave gates as you find them.
e. Leave machinery and farm animals alone, beware of the bull means just that.

Damage.
a. Litter and Food. Take your litter and left over food home with you. This can be dangerous to wildlife and farm animals by spreading disease. It is also a criminal offence.
b. Take care around plants, trees and rocks, not to damage or take them. They could be a wildlife habitat, and let others enjoy their beauty.
c. Wild and farm animals can be unpredictable, so give them plenty of room.
d. Fires can cause death and destruction to people, wildlife, farm animals, and property. Be careful that you leave nothing behind that could cause a fire, such as glass by magnifying the sun. Do not discard lit cigarette ends. If you do see any fire that is not controlled then telephone 999.

Pet Control.
a. The law. You must control your dog at all times so that it will not scare or disturb wildlife or farm animals. Farmers are entitled to destroy a dog that injures or worries their animals

b. In the event of being chased by a farm animal, then let your dog go and protect yourself. Your dog will run much faster than you.

c. A general rule is to keep your dog on a lead, there are certain periods in the year, such as the lambing season, and when young farm animals are around.

d. Dog Mess. Clean up your dog's mess and discard it in the correct way. Everyone knows just how bad dog mess is. Make sure your dog is wormed regularly.

Consideration.

The majority of people that access the country do so by car. Ensure:

> You do not block any access to gateways, driveways, farms and fields.
> Drive slowly along the narrow country roads. You never know what is around the bend or over the rise.

For more information visit: www.countryaccess.gov.uk

SECTION 1

RIPON

LOCATION

Ripon lies in North Yorkshire, north of Leeds and Harrogate close to the A1M, between the Yorkshire Dales National Park and the North York Moors National Park. Sitting at an approximate altitude of 22 to 45 metres above sea level, this small city has been established along the river Skell, a tributary that flows into the river Ure. The river Ure fringes the City on its Eastern flank. The location of Ripon gains a limited amount of protection from the weather by being relatively close to the Pennines, making the climate, in my eyes, moderate throughout most of the year.

HISTORY

Ripon is a city of considerable historical interest and for historical facts within its bounds. The Cathedral is Ripon's centre piece attraction and has a large foothold in the history of the city. Well worth a visit, you can try to unravel how and when it was built. It is filled with many beautiful features namely its architecture and stained glass windows.

In 1836 the church changed from a Minster to a Cathedral and with the arrival and appointment of the first Bishop, Bishop Langley the diocese of Ripon was created. In the crypt you will discover the remnants of St Wilfrid's Church that dates back to 672 AD.

Main Entrance to the Cathedral

The Cathedral holds many functions, mainly classical, throughout the year, with musical performances from renowned orchestras providing the general public with an opportunity to indulge in an atmosphere of outstanding splendour.

Today the Cathedral, like any building needs care and constant maintenance, that requires much needed money. Your visit could help.

SANCTUARY

In the year 924AD King Aethelstan granted Sanctuary to the church of Ripon. The sanctuary boundary was deemed to be approximately 1 mile from all sides of the church, marked by stones with a cross marked on them. This meant that any individual that entered inside the sanctuary area would be granted sanctuary by the church. This did not mean that the individual got away scot free, but would at some time go on trial before the church, where discipline could range from anything, assisting in the church for a period of time to excommunication. This type of sanctuary only lasted up until the 1500's.

Original Sanctuary Marker Stone
Sharow

Today new Sanctuary marker stones, except one original, have been placed out by the Ripon Rotary Club and the Ripon Rotary Rowels. They provide a walk around the ancient boundary of the City measuring approximately 10 miles, where you can either make the route a series of short walks, or just do the whole thing. At any point along the walk you are never that far from the City Centre where refreshments and shelter can be found.

New Sanctuary Stone 2005
at Hewick Bridge

Direction Sign

Information

Standing outside the Tourist Information Office, opposite the Cathedral, you will find the plaque about The Sanctuary Way, inside you can be provided with a leaflet guide to help you around. However the next few pages give a detailed description of the route

RIPON
THE SANCTUARY STONES WALK

RIPON CATHEDRAL to HEWICK BRIDGE - STONE 1

1. From Ripon Cathedral, facing the main entrance, turn right through the graveyard along the footpath. Go down the steps under the arch, and at the road turn left passing the house with the round windows, to the road junction.

2. At the road junction turn right and head straight on crossing the footbridge over the River Skell, by the Water Rat public house.
3. Turn left over the footbridge and follow the footpath next to the river, initially, then by road passing a line of houses on the right, and onto the footpath, straight on to the river junction with the River Ure.
4. Follow the footpath round to the right that runs parallel with the River Ure, all the way along to the path junction with the road at Hewick Bridge.
5. Turn left and cross the bridge, taking care of the busy traffic on this road. Then turn immediately left onto a footpath where the 1st Sanctuary marker stone stands.

Route to Sharow

Distance: 2.4 km. Approximate Time: 32 minutes.

HEWICK BRIDGE STONE 1 to SHAROW CROSS - STONE 2

The only remaining original Sanctuary Cross.

1. Pass the Hewick Bridge marker stone and continue along the footpath for a short distance where the footpath crosses a field diagonally to a wood and a field boundary with a metal gate.
2. Turn right through the gate and follow the footpath that fringes a wood on the right to its end, where the footpath joins a track and bears left.
3. Continue along the track to its end, where it meets the road in Sharow.
4. Turn left onto the road, and follow it along up to a road junction where you will find the 2nd Sanctuary marker stone, which is National Trust owned.
Distance: 2.3 km. Approximate Time: 28 minutes

<u>SHAROW CROSS STONE 2 to A61 HUTTON HILL FARM - STONE 3 (Not on the Route)</u>

For those wishing to visit this stone, though it is not recommended, and well out of your way:

1. Turn left at the road junction where the Sharow Cross lies, and using the pavement follow the road downhill and round the bend. Then cross the road and take the footpath that goes underneath the bypass to North Bridge mini roundabout.

2. Turn right and head uphill passing Ripon Landrover showroom and garage on the left for 1.1 km. Next to Hutton Hill Farm stands Marker stone 3.

Distance: 1.7 km. Approximate Time: 23 minutes

SHAROW CROSS STONE 3 to RIPON GOLF CLUB – STONE 4

Route avoiding Hutton Hill Farm Marker Stone 3.

1. Turn left at the road junction on to Dishforth Road, and using the pavement follow the road downhill and round the bend, cross the road and take the footpath that goes underneath the bypass road to North Bridge.

2. Turn left and cross North Bridge over the River Ure. Info: Refreshments can be taken at Fresh Fields Farm shop next to The Station pub, tea, coffee and sandwiches.

3. Turn right down River View road after crossing the bridge and follow the road to a complex of wooden buildings on the right; Riverside Leisure & Atrium Leisure.

4. Follow the road round to the right passing Atrium Leisure and passing the tennis courts on the left to a gate and the start of the footpath.

5. Follow the footpath that runs alongside the river, crossing stiles then through into a field that has no gate, finally to a stile in the corner by the wood.

6. Cross the stile and follow the path up that fringes a wood on the right, eventually dropping down to a corner of a field. The footpath cuts diagonally across up through the field to South Parks Farm.

7. At the farm the footpath ends; you continue on a road that runs through the middle of the farm to a junction.

8. Turn left at the junction and follow the road that divides the Golf course greens to its end with the main road.

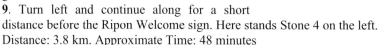

View of South Parks Farm

9. Turn left and continue along for a short distance before the Ripon Welcome sign. Here stands Stone 4 on the left.

Distance: 3.8 km. Approximate Time: 48 minutes

RIPON GOLF CLUB STONE 4 to KIRKBY ROAD/CEMETARY – STONE 5

1. At Stone 4 continue on towards Ripon for 250 metres until you see a farm track on the right, the footpath.
2. Turn right on to the footpath/track and head straight for 300 metres to a field boundary hedge with trees. Do not cross in to the next field but turn left and follow the path along to a concealed gate along the field boundary in a corner. Go through this gate stile and follow the path to the end, where you will find Stone 5 by the cemetery.
Distance: 1.4 km. Approximate Time: 17 minutes

KIRKBY ROAD/CEMETERY STONE 5 to HELL WATH – STONE 6

1. Turn right at the road with Stone 5 and walk up Kirkby Road to the post box to Lark Lane on the left.
2. Turn left down Lark Lane to its end with a road junction. Here on the left is a post office Co-op shop.
3. Turn right at the road junction and cross over the road to walk up to Bishopton Lane.
4. Turn left down Bishopton Lane and follow it downhill, bending left and eventually onto a distinctive road junction close to the bridge that crosses the River Laver.
5. Turn right at the road junction and cross the bridge following the road along to a footpath on the left, just past a wooded area on the left.
6. Cross the road and access the footpath through the gate/stile, following the footpath to a footpath crossing.
7. Turn left at the footpath crossing and follow the footpath along crossing a small stone footbridge and shortly after to a gate stile. Continue on over a small rise to a second stream bridge. The footpath rises up to a stile and ends where Stone 6 Stands.
Distance: 3.5 km. Approximate Time: 42 minutes

HELL WATH STONE 6 to QUARRY MOOR – STONE 7

1. Join the road and pass Hell Wath house on the left up to a road junction.
2. Follow the road straight on up to a cross roads, and go straight across on to West Lane.
3. Follow West lane along with houses on the left and a field edge on the right to where the road bends left. Here, as the road bends there is a footpath to the rear of the houses, running along the field edge.
4. Turn on to the footpath that runs initially at the back of the houses to some large trees where the footpath turns left. Continue along always bearing left to the car park at Quarry Moor where Stone 7 stands.
Distance: 1.2 km. Approximate Time: 15 minutes

QUARRY MOOR STONE 7 to GALLOWS HILL – STONE 8

1. Leave the car park at Quarry Moor, turn left at the road passing McDonalds and the Petrol station. Cross the road and pass Morrisons super market entrance to the traffic lights.
Info: Refreshments can be taken here at McDonalds
2. At the traffic lights turn right down Quarry Moor lane, and go past Greystones school, and at the pedestrian crossing turn immediately right up some steps on to the footpath.
3. Follow the footpath along to its end to Gallows Hill. Here you will find standing Stone 8.
Distance: 900 metres
Approximate Time: 11 minutes

GALLOWS HILL STONE 8 to RIPON CATHEDRAL

1. Join the road at Gallows Hill and turn left, over the rise then follow the road down that runs alongside the sports pitches on the right, to a road junction.
2. Turn right at the road junction and follow the road down to a large White House on the opposite side of the road, on the corner.
3. Cross the road at the white house, passing it to your right, then carry on down Bondgate to the bridge over the River Skell, passing the roundabout, and up to the Cathedral.
Distance: 1.3 km. Approximate Time: 16 minutes.

Total Distance Less Stone 3: = 16.8 km
Total Approximate Time, Less Stone 3 = 3 hrs 45 minutes

Note:

All times quoted are without breaks.

New Sanctuary
Marker Stones

16

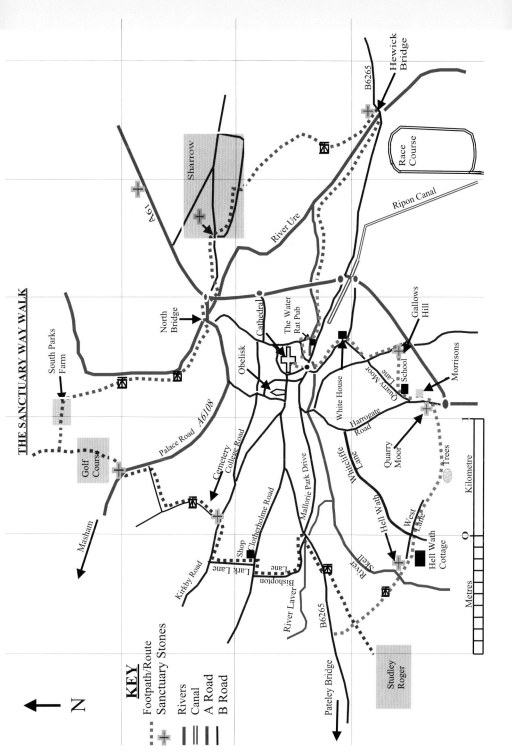

THE SANCTUARY WAY WALK

KEY

Footpath/Route
Sanctuary Stones

Rivers
Canal
A Road
B Road

N

17

RIPON TODAY

The population was averaged at 15,930 in 2003, and today the City continues to develop and grow making the City an ideal place to stay or visit on your travels. This quaint attractive place has everything to offer with its shops cafe/tea bars and restaurants that can cater for everyone's needs.

In the market square you will find the Obelisk, known as the earliest free-standing obelisk in the country, built by John Aislable of Studley Royal in 1702 replacing an earlier mediaeval market cross. Here in the Market square two ancient traditions are carried out. **The Horn Blower Ceremony**. Every night without fail a horn is blown at 2100 hrs at the four corners of the Obelisk. Then the Horn blower tells the story of the horn blower that is very interesting, drawing visitors from all over the world.

The Bellman. At 1100 hrs on Thursday a hand bell wrings out to proclaim the market is open.

Town Hall

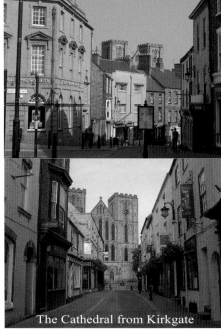

The Market Square Obelisk

The Cathedral from Kirkgate

Tourist Information. Located opposite the Cathedral.
Open: Winter, 1 Oct - 31 Mar
Thu & Sat 1000 - 1600 hrs.
Summer: 1 Apr - 3 Sept. Mon - Sat
1000 - 1700 hrs. Sun. 1300 - 1600 hrs
Tel 0845 389 0178

MUSEUMS

The museums of Ripon are an asset to the City's background and attractions, an education or a reminder of how things were and just how lucky we all are today, not to be living in those harsh times.

The Old Court House. From the moment you enter and look around and start to read the detail of history around you, you are immediately transported back in time to events that are fascinating and unbelievable compared to the punishments in our time today. Men, women and children of both sexes from 10 years of age were dealt with for minor offences such as, stealing coal to an apple, and in some cases awarded 7 years transportation to Australia. Of course more serious offences were dealt more harshly with the death penalty

The House of Correction. This building was a jail, and in its cells you will find fascinating accounts of how prisoners were treated. Restraint methods, time wasting punishments, exercise and a brief history of prisoners and the police force all here within these walls. Today prisoners have rights that were not available in those early days in the House of Correction. Today, a prisoner has a television in his or her cell and is not forced to do anything.

The Work House. The workhouse served the community in many ways, and helped the needy in hard times, because there was nothing else. Desperate people in desperately hard times, however, Ripon provided it's own remedy to the situation. The daily meals allocated in the workhouse were only a snack compared to todays standard of meals.
Could the needy and vagrants live in such a place today?

Thorpe Prebend House

The rear of Thorpe Prebend House is pictured right, and backs on to the River Skell and Bondgate. Standing below the Cathedral this is one of Ripon's oldest buildings now a museum which played host to royal visitors in its time. Here you can tour the building at leisure and discover the history of Ripon and some of its important people and visitors. A very interesting place to visit that opens at 1300 hrs daily.

RIPON CANAL

Ripon is the most northerly point on the English canal system. The Canal runs for two miles from the Ripon basin to the junction with the River Ure, utilizing three locks along its course. The Canal opened in 1773 to link the city to the navigable stretch of the River Ure, and via the Ouse to the Humber. Barges took goods out including lead and bricks, and returned with coal. This was a fast way of transportation until a quicker and cheaper system opened up, the Leeds and Thirsk Railway in 1848.

Today the Ripon Canal is home for some small boats and barge users, and for others a holiday stop in this northern point. For the people of Ripon the canal provides a place to relax and go fishing, and for others an ideal place for short walk along its banks.

BARS - INNS & PUBS.

The Unicorn

Ye Hornblower

The Black Bull

The White Horse

The Station

The Magdalens

The One Eyed Rat

They stand along the roads with colourful and interesting names, interesting and eye catching to the traveller or resident where each one holds stories to be told from past to present. They are a focal point for the local or visiting public with each one attracting different people from different backgrounds and occupations, with interior designs falling into two categories: **Fun Pubs,** Entertaining with loud music and scattered plasma TV's. **Local Original Pubs,** Community style pubs that are comfortable and relaxing and where you can have a conversation.

It is said, " You don't know a place unless you have visited every pub". There are 19 Pubs around the centre of Ripon, and to help you around them there are two Pub crawls that you can try out, one at a time, taking only half a beer in each and a pint in your favourite. Pub_**Crawl One**. Start at the **Unicorn** in the market Place, (**2**) turn right out of the Unicorn to the **ye Hornblower**, (**3**) turn right and cross the road to **The Black Bull**, (**4**) turn right out of the Black Bull and turn right crossing the road down to **The White Horse**, (**5**) turn left out of the White Horse, cross the road and walk down to **The Station,** just before North bridge, (**6**) turn right out of the Station and just before North Bridge turn right down Magdalens road to **The Magdalens** Pub on the corner, (**7**) Turn right out of the Magdalens and walk up to the cross roads with traffic lights, turn right and walk up Allhallowgate to **The One Eyed Rat**, (**8**) turn right out of the One Eyed Rat and continue up the road to **The Golden Lion**, (**9**) turn left out of the Golden Lion and walk up the road to the main junction and turn left, walk down passing Woolworth's shop to an Archway next to Boots Chemist, go through the Archway and follow the path straight through the car park to the road, turn right to the **King William 1V.**

King William 1V

The Golden Lion

Pub Crawl Two

The Royal Oak

The Water Rat

The Navigation

(1) Start in **The Royal Oak** down Kirkgate, (2) turn left out of the Royal Oak and walk around the Cathedral, down the steps and turn left to the road junction passing the house with the round windows, turn right and walk down crossing the footbridge over the River Skell to The **Water Rat**, (3) turn right out of the Water Rat and cross the main road, turn right and turn left ahead down Bondgate Green, **The Navigation** is on the left, (4) Back track out of the Navigation to the main road, turn left and at the bridge take the footpath that runs along the river to the next bridge and the road, Bondgate, turn left and walk along to **The Ship**, (5) turn left out of The Ship and walk along to the road junction at the end, by the white house, cross the road and turn right heading up keeping on this main road all the way to the road junction with the traffic lights, Harrogate Road, turn left passing McDonalds to **The Wheatsheaf** before the roundabout, (6) turn right out of The Wheatsheaf and follow the road down to the traffic lights, cross the road heading straight, not down Quarry Moor Road, all the way along to **The South Lodge** on the right side of Harrogate road, (7) turn right out of the South Lodge and follow the road into Ripon crossing the bridge and around the corner is **The Turks Head**, (8) Cross the road out of The Turks Head, to the traffic lights and turn left and walk along to **The Dog & Duck**, (9) Leave the Dog & Duck back down to the traffic lights, turn left and head up to **The Lamb & Flag** on the left, (10) turn left out of the Lamb & Flag up to the traffic lights turn left, along to **The Black Swan** on the left.

Note: From the Wheatsheaf to the South Lodge the No 36 bus could be used, that runs at regular intervals along this road.

The Ship

The Wheatsheaf

South Lodge

The Turks Head

BLACK SWAN

The Lamb & Flag

The Dog & Duck

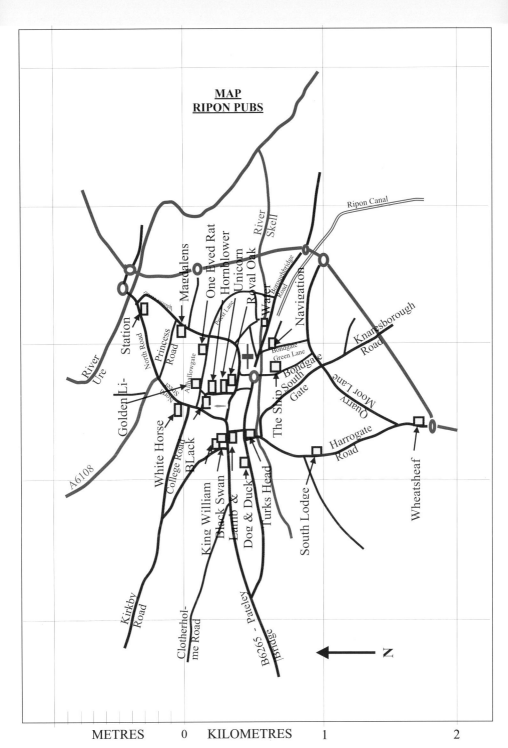

MAP
RIPON PUBS

METRES   0   KILOMETRES   1   2

RIPON RACES

Ripon's own racehorse track is just east of the city down the B6265, the Boroughbridge road, approximately 24 minutes walk from the City centre. People flock to the races from all over the country, and especially from Ripon. An ideal family day out with the Course Enclosure providing a play area for children, and a good size area for having a picnic. Entertainment is provided by the top class horses and their entourage of owners, trainers, grooms and jockeys; that have made the trip bringing their horses in the best shape possible, hopefully to win the race. The horses are paraded round a circuit to warm them up, giving the spectators an opportunity to eye them in their clean toned state, while all around is the buzz of people moving around from stands to betting offices, bars or food stands, cafeterias, and back; the whole day runs along from race to race, horses and people moving around the day. The ladies and gentleman dressed in their best clothes walk around enjoying the day.

It is, and can be a great day out, excitement and cheers can be heard all around you by the punters encouraging their horses home, hoping to win. There is plenty to choose from for catering and refreshments where you are made to feel welcome whatever your choice. Admission costs are split into three choices:

£4, Course Enclosure. This is located in the centre of the Racecourse and provides a Bar and Tea Room as well as refreshments available under cover.

£11, Tattersall Enclosure. The Grandstand and Paddock, entry to a variety of bars and Catering stands.

£17, Members Enclosure. Dress Code applies, Entry in to the Members Dining Room, and 3 Bars.
Covered seating in the Grandstand, and many other perks.

For more information see the web site: www.ripon-races.co.uk

SPA GARDENS.

They are set in the middle of Ripon, just at the end of Westgate next to the swimming baths. The gardens are maintained throughout the year with care and dedication by the gardener, with results that show everyone entering the gardens an array of colour and splendour of the flowers set just at the edge of the bowling green. There is also an impressive statue of George Frederick Samual Robinson 1st Marquess of Ripon, a War memorial, a band stand pavilion, and a crazy golf pitch for all to try there luck at. For refreshments, inside or out, the Sun Parlour Cafe provides the perfect cup of tea, cakes and light food where you can admire the flowers and greenery provided in these relaxing Gardens .

ACCOMMODATION
HOTELS
The Old Deanery Hotel & Restaurant
Minster Road, Ripon, HG4 1QS
Tel: 01765 600003
www.theoldeanery.co.uk
E:mail: reception@theolddeanery.co.uk

Ripon Spa Hotel
Park Street, Ripon, HG4 2BU
Tel: 01765 602172
www.bw-riponspahotel.co.uk
Email: spahotel@bronco.co.uk

Unicorn Hotel
Market Place, Ripon, HG4 1BP
Tel: 01765 602202
www.unicorn-hotel.co.uk/
Email: reservations@unicorn-hotel.co.uk

Inns
Black Swan
21 Westgate, Ripon, HG4 2BQ
Tel: 01765 602985

Golden Lion Inn
69-70 Allhallowgate, Ripon, North Yorkshire, HG4 1LE
Tel: 01765 602598

The Royal Oak
6 Kirkgate, Ripon, North Yorkshire, HG4 1PB
Tel: 01765 602284

The Ship
Bondgate, Ripon
Tel: 01765 603254

White Horse
61 North Street, Ripon, North Yorkshire, HG4 1EN
Tel: 01765 603622
www.white-horse-ripon.co.uk

B&Bs / GUEST HOUSE

Crescent Lodge42 North Street, Ripon, North Yorkshire, HG4 1EN
Telephone: 01765 609589

Email: malcolm@crescentlodge.co.uk

The Riverside
20/21 Boroughbridge Road, Ripon, HG4 1QW
Tel: 01765 603864
Email: christopher.pearson@virgin.net

BISHOPTON GROVE HOUSE
Ripon, HG4 2QL
01765 600888
Email: wimpress@bronco.co.uk

PLACES TO EAT

All the Hotels, Inns and Pubs mentioned will provide food at different levels of price and standards. My favourites are as follows:

<u>The Old Deanery</u>. This old building set adjacent to the Cathedral provides food and wine of a standard of excellence, and whatever the occasion, the Old Deanery can provide the perfect place for; morning or afternoon tea/coffee taken inside or out in a walled garden, or utilising the comfortable surrounds one can expect in a high standard establishment. You will be totally at ease here, assured that all food is freshly prepared and cooked to perfection. Bookings preferred but not essential, contact details for bookings are listed under the accommodation page.

Price Range: Lunch 1 Course £7.50. 2 Courses £12.50. Dinner: 2 Courses £19.50. 3 Courses £24.50 or the choice from the a la carte menu.

Lockwoods Cafe/Restaurant

83 North Street, Ripon., Tel: 01765 607555. This Cafe/Restaurant provides an atmosphere of charm and comfort amongst a new style setting in the centre of Ripon. Whatever your needs from tea/coffee, breakfast, lunch, dinner or just a snack, whatever, you can relax and pass the time of day and eat excellent food cooked in an open view kitchen for all to see. This place is good with an ever changing exciting menu providing dishes that will satisfy your taste. Price range:
Nibbles: £4.50 - £8.00. Starters:£5.95 - £6.50. Main: £7.50 - £11.50. Side Orders: £2.50 - £2.95

Perk Up Restaurant

43 Market Place, Ripon, Tel: 01765 698 888. A cosy comfortable Cafe/Restaurant, where you can take refreshments dining inside or out on the unique court yard terrace. Perk Up is all fresh on site prepared cooked food that provides a choice of excellent English style dishes. Price range:
Lunch: £3.15 - £7.50. Dinner: Starters, £5.75 - £8.95. Main: £14.95 - £19.50. Dessert: £5.95 - £7.50. Bookings advisable Telephone 01765 698888 or visit:
www.perkup.co.uk/reservation

The Ripon Spa Hotel

Park Street, Ripon. Tel 01765 690770. This Ripon prestigious hotel is 100 years old this year 2007. Yes a celebratory year for this fine beautiful spacious hotel set in the middle of Ripon. It has the Turf Tavern bar where you can indulge in bar type meals priced at £2.50 - £11.95 or you could take morning or afternoon tea/coffee on the terrace overlooking the gardens. For the more elaborate formal menu and setting you could try the main hotel restaurant, which has a high ceiling and light decorations that looks out over the gardens, and the croquet lawns. A beautiful setting in elegant surroundings. Price range: 2 Courses £17.95. 3 Courses £21.50

Prima.
Located down Kirkgate this Italian restaurant is very inviting and is always full. Proof of the good quality and reasonable priced selection of food and wine on offer. Bookings are advisable, to avoid disappointment Tel: 01765 602034

The Unicorn Hotel.
Located in the Market place, this family run hotel is full of character and history, that provides you with two stories to investigate for yourself. 1st the story of Tom Crud and 2nd the story of the ghost. The hotel provides a full menu of choice in the restaurant or you can take food in the bar area that overlooks the centre of Ripon. Tel: 01765 602202

Valentinos.
Located at the end of Westgate. Directions, standing facing the Town Hall in the market square, turn right and head straight, Valentinos stands at the end of this small Street. It is an Italian restaurant that has plenty of space and a large choice of food from its menu. Tel 01765604201

There are other places to eat at in Ripon, Chinese, English and Indian restaurants alike for you to discover, and besides those, an ample supply of cafes around the centre, though all those mentioned do provide a service where you can indulge in snacks, tea/coffee.

Spa Gardens early morning summer 2006

PLACES TO VISIT

FOUNTAINS ABBEY

This is Britain's largest monastic ruin that lies just 3 miles north of Ripon along the river Skell. Fountains Abbey & Studley Royal has been owned by the National Trust since 1983. In 1986 Studley Royal incorporating the ruins of Fountains Abbey was designated a World Heritage Site.

Within the 760 acre estate is: a 12th century Cistercian abbey and Watermill, an 18th century pleasure garden and a large deer park, which is home to three species of deer, about 550 in number.

There is also a Tudor house within the abbey precincts and a Victorian, Gothic revival, church in the deer park. A magnificent 18th century, Palladian style, stable block can be glimpsed across the deer park but unfortunately cannot be visited as it is a private residence.

Private tours of the abbey and gardens are offered during the summer months (April to October) and audio tours of the abbey will shortly become available. This. Is well worth a full day's visit.

Today Fountains Abbey is one of my favourite places to visit, and for many others too, with visitors each year over 300,000. The National Trust are today's guardians of this historical site, that have provided parking, access, cafe's and National Trust shops to cater for all your needs during your visit. Getting there, Monday - Saturday the 139 Ripon Roweller Bus: Ripon Bus Station: 1030, 1320 & 1535 hrs - Out Going Fountains Abbey Visitors Centre: 1050, 1417 & 1547 hrs - Back to Ripon.

Contact: www.fountainsabbey.org.uk. Email. info@fountainsabbey.org.uk. Tel. 01765 608888.

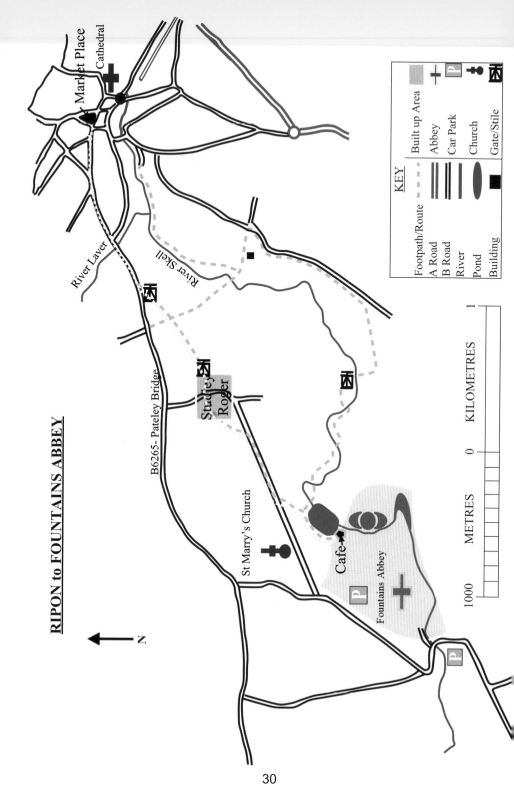

RIPON to FOUNTAINS ABBEY

Market Place
Cathedral

River Laver

River Skell

B6265- Pateley Bridge

Studley Roger

St Marry's Church

Cafe

Fountains Abbey

N

KEY

Footpath/Route
A Road
B Road
River
Pond
Building

Built up Area
Abbey
Car Park
Church
Gate/Stile

METRES   KILOMETRES

1000   0   1

LIGHTWATER VALLEY

Lightwater Valley is a theme and amusement park packed with things to do and rides to try out for all the family. Enjoyment is the parks main feature for all who enter its grounds. Everybody is catered for from small children to adults, nursery play area rides to white knuckle rides for the taller people and thrills seekers. Everything is here even nature trails to explore. Not forgetting the abundant places to eat and rest or gather yourself before the next ride or adventure. The entrance greets you with a small area of shops close to the Bird of Prey Centre. Peoples excited cries and screams can be heard over the neighbouring fields and countryside, carrying across to North Stainley and Middle Parks farm. Lightwater Valley is located on the northern doorstep of Ripon, just a few miles north and just before the village of North Stainley along the A6108.

Getting there: the 159 bus service stops at Lightwater Valley (LWV) Monday - Saturday at the following times:
Ripon - LWV: 0935, 1140, 1340, 1535, 1730 hrs
LWV - Ripon: 0912, 1112, 1310, 1715 hrs

Contact:www.lightwatervalley.co.uk.el.
E-mail. leisure@lightwatervalley.co.uk. Tel.0870 458 0040
Top Tip. To get the cheapest price on a ticket for entry, and in advance of your visit, buy your ticket on line. Go to:
http://www.lastminute.com
Click on Going Out, Click on Theme Parks, Click Lightwater Valley

31

NEWBY HALL

Located 2 miles from the A1 road, North of Harrogate lying between the historic City of Ripon and Boroughbridge along the River Ure.

Newby Hall was built in the 17th century, but today it is a family home open to the public to share its grandness and beauty in its tranquil setting.

Today it is a great day out for all, providing the grandness and splendour of the Hall, the many featured gardens and walks such

as the Sculpture Park through woodland. For the children there is the adventure Garden and paddling pool next to the miniature railway ride and additionally there are boat trips along the river. Here you can find yourself totally at ease, able to relax and enjoy the sights and tranquillity in this beautiful setting, not forgetting the provision of refreshments inside or out at the restaurant. A must for a visit.

Contact: Newby Hall & Gardens,
Estate Office, Newby Hall, Ripon, North Yorkshire, HG4 5AE.
www.newbyhall.com.
Tel. 0845 4504068

SECTION 2
THE RIPON ROWEL
RIPON to WEST TANFIELD

Transport. The 159 Bus operates a regular service Monday - Saturday only at the following times from West Tanfield: 0909 1109 1307 1509 1712 hrs.
The bus stop is opposite The Bull Inn.
Total Distance: 11.3 km
Total Time: 2 hrs 17 minutes, without breaks.
1145 hrs is an option to start. This enables you to take advantage of lunch at the Staveley Arms in North Stainley and still catch the 1509 hrs bus back to Ripon.

Ripon Market Place to River View Road (North Bridge).
(**1**) Start in the Market square with your back to the town hall and walk up the road passing Boots and Woolworths shops down North Street to the Clock Tower.
(**2**) Cross the road by the Clock Tower and head straight on down North Road passing the post office shop on the left, dropping down toward North Bridge and River View Road on the left.
Distance: 1 km, Time 12 minutes.
Info: The Clock Tower was built in 1897 to commemorate Queen Victoria's diamond jubilee, and inaugurated in 1898, as stated on the plaque

River View Road to South Parks Farm.
(**1**) Turn left down River View Road and follow it along passing the river side lodgings, wooden buildings, and Atrium Health & Leisure club on the right. The road ascends then bends left turning into a track just before a gate/stile ahead.
(**2**) Pass through the gate and continue along the footpath that runs alongside the River Ure for some distance to a gate/stile. Continue on eventually into a final field where the path runs into a corner to a gate/stile by a wood.
(**3**) Pass through the gate/stile and follow the footpath up fringing the wood on the right, then dropping down to the corner of a field where the footpath crosses it diagonally up to South Parks Farm. Follow the footpath around the bungalow and join the farm road that runs straight through the farm.
Distance : 1.8 km, Time 24 minutes.

Above: Footpath to South Parks Farm

33

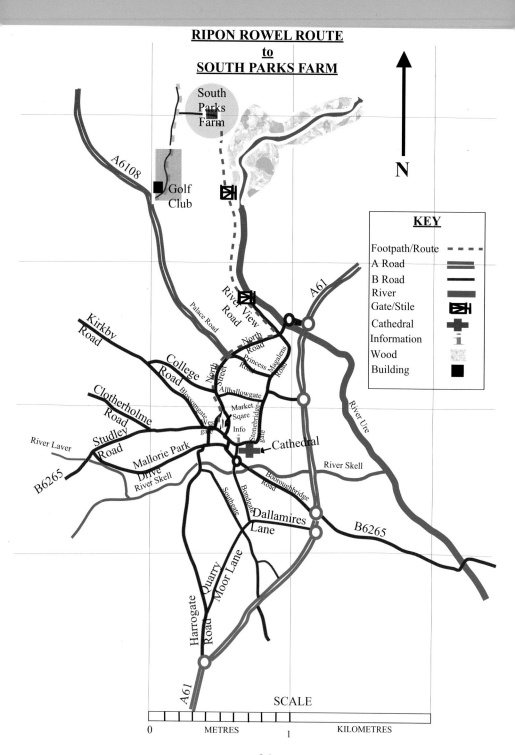

RIPON ROWEL ROUTE
to
SOUTH PARKS FARM

South Parks Farm to Middle Parks Farm.

(**1**) Walk down the road that runs straight through South Parks farm down to a road junction, turn right and continue along bearing left at the Y junction ahead. You are now in a Military Training Area, though you seldom see any soldiers here. Continue along the road all the way passing the Fishing Ponds on the right up to Middle Parks Farm.

Distance : 2 km, Time 22 minutes

Middle Parks Farm to North Parks Farm.

(**1**) At the Farm bear left over the cattle grid and follow the road along that by passes Middle Parks farm.

(**2**) Continue along the road to where the road bends sharply to the left.

(**3**) Head straight here cutting the corner, do not bear left, and continue on up to North Parks Farm: 1.2 km, Time: 14 minutes.

North Parks Farm to North Stainley.

North Parks Farm

(**1**) At the farm, head straight on to the gate that stand close to the farm house.

(**2**) Go through the gate into the field and follow path straight to a wooden gate/stile ahead.

(**3**) Go through the gate/stile and join the track that runs along side High Batts Nature Reserve on the right, to a hard core track ahead.

(**4**) Turn left at the track and continue on until the track turns left ahead with a small track leading off on the right with a footpath direction sign.

(**5**) Turn right and walk down this track for some distance, eventually gaining your first glimpses of North Stainley on the left across the fields. Carry on until you pass under some power lines, and straight after at the edge of the wood on your left, after a very shortly distance, turn left down a footpath that will lead you to North Stainley and the Staveley Arms.

Distance: 1.7 km, Time: 20 minutes

NORTH STAINLEY

This small village is situated along the A6108 approximately 4 miles north of Ripon. The first building you come across on the right is The Stavelely Arms, open from 1200 hrs daily providing refreshments from a simple drink and a sandwich to a full 3 course meal. Other attractions in the village are the cricket ground, the venue for many a car boot sale on Bank holidays, and the little church opposite. In the village, just past the Staveley Arms is a village garage shop/post office,

The Staveley Arms

which is useful to know to purchase small items for your travels.

North Stainley to Sleningford Watermill Caravan & Camping Park.

(1) At The Staveley Arms turn right and follow the road through the village of North Stainley, passing the cricket ground and church and exit the village.

(2) Continue along following the road until you pass two roads on the left signed Mickley. Shortly after these roads you come across a gate and a track on the right.

(3) Pass through the gate and follow the track to its end by the Mill Batts Wood and a gate stile.

(4) Pass through the gate and turn left down a grassed track that runs alongside a wood then down into Sleningford Watermill Caravan & Camping Park and to the Shop building.

Distance: 2 km, Time: 24 minutes

SLENINGFORD WATERMILL CARAVAN & CAMPING PARK

The Site is about halfway between North Stainley and West Tanfield situated along the river next to Mill Batts Wood. The main site building provides you with another opportunity to relax and purchase some basic items and refreshments at the shop and there also you can enjoy the scenery along the river.

MAP
ROUTE to NORTH STAINLEY

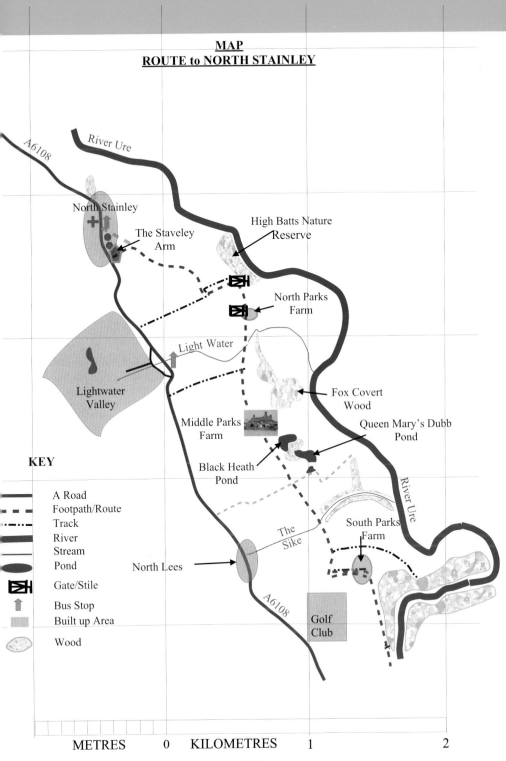

KEY

- ▬▬▬ A Road
- - - - Footpath/Route
- ·—·—· Track
- ▬▬▬ River
- ═══ Stream
- ⬭ Pond
- ⋈ Gate/Stile
- ⬆ Bus Stop
- ▦ Built up Area
- ⬬ Wood

River Ure

A6108

North Stainley

The Staveley Arm

High Batts Nature Reserve

North Parks Farm

Light Water

Lightwater Valley

Fox Covert Wood

Middle Parks Farm

Queen Mary's Dubb Pond

Black Heath Pond

North Lees

The Sike

South Parks Farm

River Ure

A6108

Golf Club

METRES   0   KILOMETRES   1   2

Sleningford Water Mill Caravan & Camping Park to West Tanfield.

(1) Follow the park site road out to where the entrance road bears left and the footpath leaves the road to join the river.

(2) Turn slightly right and take the footpath that runs alongside the river.

(3) Follow the footpath alongside the river all the way around to the bridge at West Tanfield.

(4) Turn right, cross the bridge into West Tanfield.

Distance: 1.6 km, Time: 20 minutes

WEST TANFIELD

West Tanfield is situated along the River Ure approximately 6 miles NW of Ripon along the A6108 road. As soon as you approach the village at the bridge you come across a picture perfect image of a row of stone cottages whose gardens terrace down to the river in lavish greenery. While at the back of the cottages is the church of St Nicholas, well worth a visit. This is filled with ancient memorials, tombs and artefacts. Next to the church is the historic Marmion Tower where you can ascend up to view the surrounding area. There is a school and a post office, but the eye catcher is The Bull Inn, the first building you meet once crossing the bridge into West Tanfield on the left, here you can eat in or out or just have a drink and enjoy watching the river go by from its terrace garden.

Accommodation & Places to Eat

Bruce Arms Bistro, West Tanfield, Yorkshire, HG4 3JJ. Tel: 01677 470325. Food only.

The Bull Inn, West Tanfield, Ripon HG4 5JQ. Tel: 01677 470678. Provides accommodation and good food.

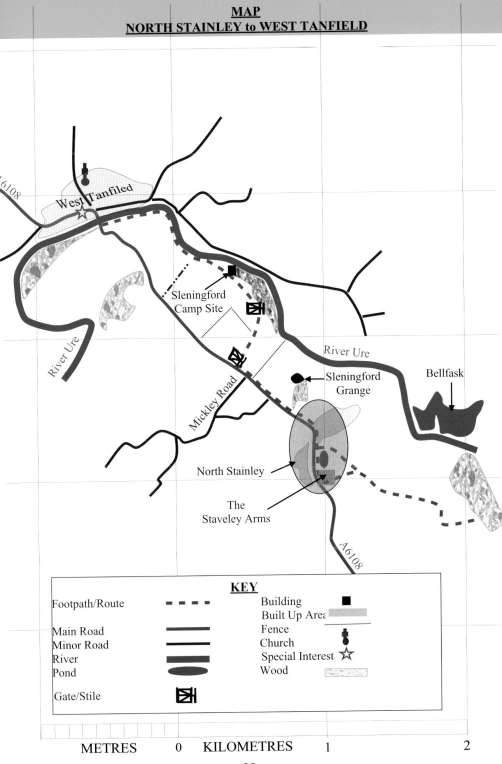

MAP
NORTH STAINLEY to WEST TANFIELD

6108

West Tanfiled

Sleningford
Camp Site

River Ure

River Ure

Mickley Road

Sleningford
Grange

Bellfask

North Stainley

The
Staveley Arms

A6108

KEY

Footpath/Route	- - - -	Building	■
		Built Up Area	
Main Road		Fence	
Minor Road		Church	
River		Special Interest	☆
Pond		Wood	
Gate/Stile			

METRES   0   KILOMETRES   1   2

SECTION 3
THE RIPON ROWEL
WEST TANFIELD - MASHAM

West Tanfield to Mickley.

(**1**) Cross over the bridge that spans the River Ure and walk down the signed footpath/track that leads to Quarry House farm. Just before the house cross the stile next to the footpath sign.

Quarry House Field Crossing

(**2**) Follow the fence on the left up to a stile, then without crossing it bear right and cross the field diagonally to the corner by the river, and a gate that enters the wood.

(**3**) Go through the gate and follow the footpath that rises and falls, but runs parallel to the river. The footpath eventually leaves the wood by an overgrown vegetation area, twisting and turning along its course, over level ground close to the river, eventually passing a new plantation field on the left and then an open field.

(**4**) Continue along and you will see buildings ahead, slightly left, this is Old Sleningford farm. The path rises at an earth bank that is a mix of shrubs and edges plants that mark this field boundary. The footpath continues on crossing another field close to the river, before entering a wood below the farm.

(**5**) As you enter the wood the path splits, go left slightly into the wood and the path drops down to a small stream that you cross over a flag stone.

(**6**) Cross the stream and cross in to the field that exits the wood.

(**7**) With the wood on the right and fields on your left continue on along until you see a gate and a break between the woods. Go through the gate and follow the wall on the left to the corner, here you will see a line of trees that cross the open field all the way to a gate/stile that enters into Mickley. Distance: 2.5 km, Approximate Time: 38 minutes

Approaching Mickley

MICKLEY

Located, South West of West Tanfield, North West of North Stainley, it is accessed from the A6108 signed Mickley/Kirkby Malzeard, just north of North Stainley. This small lovely village has a road lined with trees running through it, with stone cottages with big gardens along its route. Here the village backs onto the the River Ure, where you will discover.

River Ure - rear of Mickley

Mickleys secret, the old mill and mill race that separates a thin stretch of land from the main river bank, providing picturesque scenery and short walks along its banks. Just walk along the main road through Mickley to the last house and turn right.

Mickley to Fisher's Hall Ruin.

(**1**) Walk up the track to the main road in Mickley and turn right. Then walk down the footpath the full length of Mickley, passing the little church St Johns on the right, to the last house on the right. Follow the road uphill passing the farm on the left, to a slight bend and a small gravel area on the right, to the footpath entering the wood.

(**2**) Enter the wood and follow the footpath along, the path rises and falls, then meets some steps and a direction sign.

Mickley Road

(**3**) Go up the steps and follow the footpath up that runs close to the wood edge. After this the footpath is up and down then meets a footpath direction sign with a path coming in from sharp left.

(**4**) Bear right at this direction post and continue on to meet two muddy sections ahead. Bear right at both muddy sections along here, and do not go left and up. The path is small and narrow and heads straight.

(**5**) Ahead the path causes a little confusion entering a small clearing in the wood that is close to a field, dense with high vegetation, here a path as been made to take the best course through this section, but do not go up or cross any fences, instead head along and down to meet the fence corner to where you bear left and enter the wooded area again with the footpath running close to the edge of the wood.

(**6**) The path ahead descends slightly over its course, and eventually the ground to the left becomes steep and through the vegetation, crags can be seen.

(**7**) Shortly ahead the path crosses a wet area close to the river, and ahead meets some steps with a path either side.

(**8**) Ascend the steps and follow the path up a short distance to Fisher's Hall Ruin.

Distance: 2.7 km. Approximate Time: 42 minutes

(Fisher's Hall, above)

Information: Fisher's Hall lies close to Grewelthorpe in Hack Fall wood. It was built in 1750 by William Aislabie part of a tourist attraction then, to walk and view the scenery provided in places of the distant views of Masham church along the river. All this was managed and the tourist were charged a small fee at that time. Today it is all free.

MAP
WEST TANFIELD - FISHER'S HALL

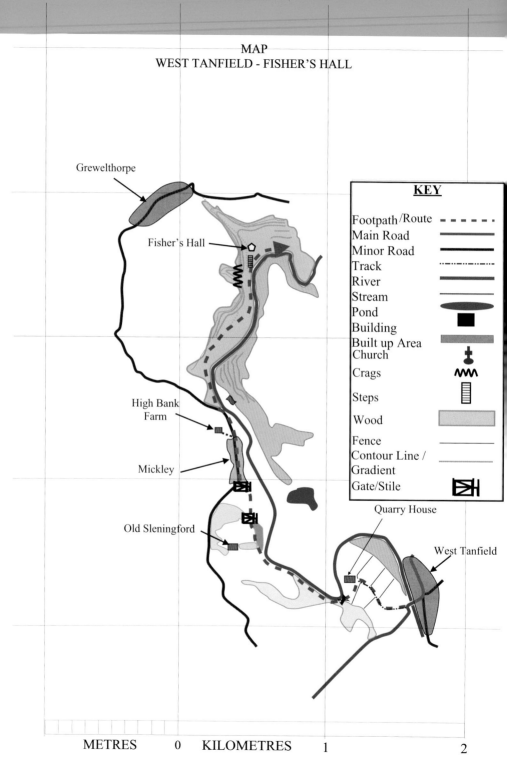

Grewelthorpe

Fisher's Hall

High Bank
Farm

Mickley

Old Sleningford

Quarry House

West Tanfield

KEY

Footpath/Route
Main Road
Minor Road
Track
River
Stream
Pond
Building
Built up Area
Church
Crags
Steps
Wood
Fence
Contour Line /
Gradient
Gate/Stile

METRES   0   **KILOMETRES**   1   2

Fisher's Hall Ruin to Low Burn Bridge.

(1) Descend down the path from Fisher's Hall Ruin and turn left, along the footpath. The path has been maintained in places along this section with boarded areas and steps that run along close to the river.

(2) Ahead you eventually come across a path junction with a marker post, bear left as directed and ascend diagonally up where the path eventually meets a gate at the top.

(3) Go through the gate that enters a field, and follow the fence line along to a second gate.

(4) Go through the gate and follow the path left and down, the path bends at the bottom and runs parallel to the river on the right.

(5) Follow the path along that meets the end of the wood ahead by a stile into fields.

(6) Cross the stile into the fields and follow the ground that runs close to the river to a gate just below Nutwith Cote Farm.

(7) Cross the gate and continue along close to the river that bends left ahead.

(8) Cross a stile following the path through a small enclosure to a hedgerow fence, then cross the next just before Badger Lane Farm.

(9) The path drops down to meet a hand rail bridge then continues along following a fence line left and the river right all the way around to the road at Low Burn Bridge.

Distance: 3.3 km. Approximate Time: 48 minutes

Low Burn Bridge to Masham.

(1) Turn right and cross Low Burn Bridge, then turn immediately right down the signed route along the River Burn.

(2) Close to where the River Burn joins the River Ure turn left up the earth steps, then turn right and follow along the footpath that fringes the fields. There are a few seat and benches along this section of the river where the footpath runs all the way along to meet the sewage works and a track.

(3) Turn left at the sewage works and follow the track up through a gate to the road. Follow the road around and up into the centre, the market place of Masham.

Distance: 2 km

Approximate Time: 25 minutes.

Transport. The 159 Ripon - Masham Bus can be used to get to West Tanfield, and return from Masham. Times from Ripon: 0935, 1140, 1340, 1535 & 1730 hrs.
Times from Masham: 0855, 1055, 1255, 1455 & 1700hrs. - Back to Ripon.

Total Distance: 10.5 km
Total Time: 2 hrs 31 minutes without breaks

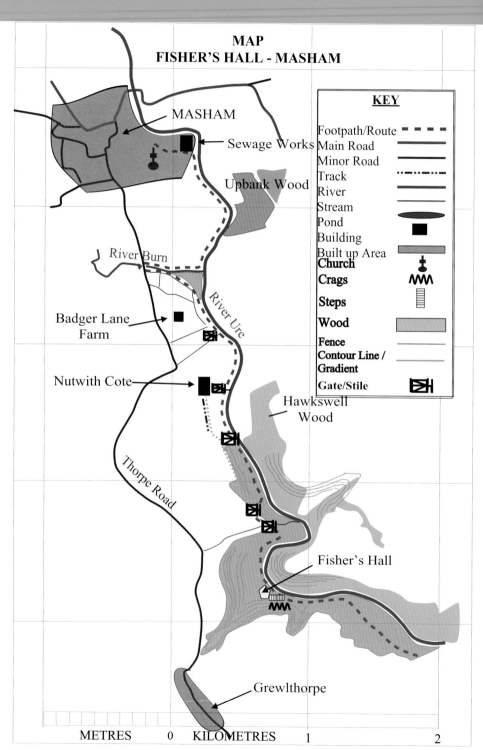

MAP
FISHER'S HALL - MASHAM

MASHAM

Sewage Works

Upbank Wood

River Burn

River Ure

Badger Lane Farm

Nutwith Cote

Hawkswell Wood

Thorpe Road

Fisher's Hall

Grewlthorpe

KEY	
Footpath/Route	- - -
Main Road	
Minor Road	
Track	
River	
Stream	
Pond	
Building	■
Built up Area	
Church	
Crags	ᴧᴧᴧ
Steps	
Wood	
Fence	
Contour Line / Gradient	
Gate/Stile	

METRES   0   KILOMETRES   1   2

44

MASHAM

Masham is the northern limit of the Ripon Rowel walk, by 10 miles, located along the A6108 next to the River Ure. A rural village with a large market place that serves the community with many fairs: The Sheep Fair, Craft Fairs, Beer festival, Victorian Christmas Fair, and the regular markets. As well there is the Steam Engine Rally, Masham Horticultural Show and many other functions that take place throughout the

year in this nice village full of quaint stone buildings and homes set along its streets.

Activities

Pony Trekking and horse riding caters for all abilities at the Highland Pony Riding Centre just outside of Masham, on the Swinton Road. Contact: Dykes Hill House, Masham, Ripon HG4 4NS
Tel: 01765 689241 **Fax**: 01765 688184
E-mail: susan@masham1935.fsnet.co.uk
Web: www.yorkshirenet.co.uk/mashamriding
Cost: £17.50 per hour. Absolute beginners welcome.

PLACES TO VISIT

Reah's Delicatessen & Bakery. This is a shop where you can have sandwiches made up from whatever is on display, cakes and all. A delicatessen that provides choices from a wide range of fine foods, chocolates and cakes. You will definitely enjoy a visit to Reah's.

Joneva. This is a confectionary/delicatessen that specialises in Belgian Chocolates, situated in the Market Place.

Web: www.joneva.com

PLACES TO STAY & EAT

HOTELS

Kings Head Hotel
Market Place, Masham
Tel: 01765 689295
Web: www.kingsheadmasham.com

This 18th Century Georgian building is located right in the centre of Masham overlooking the Market place, with wooden beams and wooden panelling giving the interior a warm homely feeling. The hotel has just been totally refurbished, so you can be sure you will feel relaxed in this atmospheric comfortable hotel, that is ideally situated, and very reasonably priced.

The food prepared and served is traditional English, where you will find Beef Wellington, duck and many more choices of that nature available.

> **Cost per Night**: £55 - £85, Breakfast not included in the price
> **Dining:** Starters Range from £2.99 - £9.99. Main Courses: £6.45 - £14.95.

Swinton Park Hotel ****

Swinton Park Hotel, Swinton, Masham, Ripon, North Yorkshire HG4 4JH.
Tel: 01765 680900
Web: www.swintonpark.com

This is a four star luxury hotel only 1 mile outside of Masham set in 200 acres of beautiful scenic grounds, containing gardens lakes and woodlands. On approaching the hotel you are captivated by the castle style stately building that stands in front of you. The interior is opulently furnished in every room, and you are made to feel comfortable in this very nice hotel. Activities can be arranged and provided here that relate to the countryside, and for those interested in cookery, there

is a cookery school where only fine food made from local produce is prepared

Cost per Night: £150 - £350, single to suites, includes breakfast. There are also special offers advertised on the website.

46

Dining. All the courses and indulgences are catered for residents and none residents.

Bar & Lounge 1100 – 2200 hrs provides light food sandwiches to a plate Style meal. Cost: £6.50 - £18.00 depending on your appetite.

Samuel's Restaurant. This grand opulent room is large with windows that provide grand views of the grounds. It is here that food of the finest quality is prepared and served to the highest standards for those that have read the words of such a desirable changing seasonal menu. This is a centre of excellence for service, food and wine; and whatever the occasion Samuel's Restaurant can make your day very special.

Lunch. Two Courses: £ 17.50. Three Courses: £21.50.

Dinner. There are two menus of choice: The Dinner Menu: a meal of three courses, Cost £39. The Tasting Menu: seven separate dishes, Cost £48, additionally £35 for the three bottles of wine chosen for you to accompany this menu.

Afternoon Tea. Served in the Drawing Room 1500 – 1800 hrs, and after seeing this room you will not want to leave. The prices are very reasonable and it is well worth visiting if only just to take tea in these settings. Cost: £7.50 upwards. Additionally you could take tea or coffee in the Bar & Lounge for £3.

Swinton Park Hotel has many choices, and should not be written off as too expensive, but, you should use the hotel for your own purposes and budget. Bookings for all the hotels provisions are required.

PUBs & GUEST HOUSES

Bay Horse Inn
Silver Street, Masham, North Yorkshire, HG4 4DX
Tel: 01765 689236
Cost for B&B En suite rooms: £25 per person per night, Weekdays. £35 per person, Weekends.
Serving basic bar type meals, lunch times only.

The Bruce Arms

3 Little Market Place, Masham.
Tel: 01765 689372
Cost B&B: £30 per person. Without Breakfast:
£25, shared facilities.
Serving basic bar type food..
Additionally The Bruce Arms has a great terrace
beer garden that overlooks the cricket pitches.

THE THEAKSTON BREWERY

The Black Bull in Paradise Brewery Visitors Centre, Masham, Ripon, North Yorkshire,
HG4 4YD.
Tel: 01765 680000. Email: bookings@theakstons.co.uk.
Web: www.theakstons.co.uk

Masham is home of the famous Theakstons Brewery one of the
proudest family breweries in Yorkshire. With its

180 year history the brewery is definitely worth a
visit. Established in 1827 by Robert Theakston
who began brewing in the Black Bull, the original
Masham Inn, before his son Thomas built the
present brewery in 1875. The traditional
Victorian brewhouse is still in operation today
and many famous beers including the legendary
Old Peculier are brewed here. Also of interest is
the working cooperage – visitors can watch the
Theakston Cooper crafting the traditional
wooden casks from a viewing window in the
Heritage Centre a rare sight as he is one of only
two craft coopers in the brewing industry today.
Wooden casks are still used by the brewery to
supply local pubs with the Old Peculier. You
don't have to search far to find the Brewery in
Masham, the aroma of brewing beer reaches you
in and around the Marketplace, to let any visitor
know what direction the brewery lies.

Today the brewery is once again family owned and aids the local
community in a wide range of charitable events, besides
providing employment for many residents in the Masham area.

The Black Bull in Paradise. This is the Brewery's Visitors
Centre and is named after the original Black Bull Inn and
Paradise fields the name of the fields where the Brewery stands
today. Here you can indulge and sample the first class beers that
are freshly served from the pump in comfortable surrounding at
your leisure.

Brewery Tours. These tours operate from the Visitors Centre at
a very reasonable price. You will learn about the ingredients and

the process of brewing beer throughout all its stages, touring the original Victorian brewhouse. You may even see the Cooper, crafting the traditional wooden barrels.

Heritage Centre. Located in the Black Bull in Paradise, where you can experience a virtual tour given by Simon Theakston by audio and visual means, and also see the many historic brewery items saved over the years.

Gift Shop. Located within the Black Bull in Paradise Visitor Centre, there is large selection of Theakston souvenirs and gifts which can be purchased.

Opening Times. Open daily:
4 January – 23 December 1030 hrs onwards. For more information contact The Black Bull in Paradise Brewery Visitors Centre stated above.

BLACK SHEEP BREWERY

Wellgarth, Masham, North Yorkshire, HG4 4EN.
Tel: 01765 680101
Web: www.blacksheepbrewery.co.uk

This Brewery is in fact only 15 years old. Established in the early nineties by Paul Theakston, 5th generation of Masham's famous brewing family, it now produces a staggering 17 million pints a year. Black Sheep Brewery uses traditional brewing methods coupled with the finest ingredients to create distinctive beers that are packed full of character and flavour.

Visitors Centre. Here you can take a guided tour of the brewery and experience the traditional brewing process, from the aroma and taste of English hops and malted barley, through to sampling one of the award-wining ales.

Bistro & Bar. This is a place where you and your family can indulge and relax, whatever the occasion. It is spacious and modern and serves refreshments from morning to evening, ranging from tea/coffee and snacks to lavish 3-course evening meals. With wonderful views over the River Ure and surrounding countryside it is definitely a unique venue to hold your private party or wedding reception.

Black Sheep Shop. From clothing to cuddly sheep, bottle openers to bottled beer, with over 1,000 different items on sale there's something for everyone. The shop can also be accessed on-line at the website address above.

The Black Sheep Brewery has outstanding facilities. This is a must to visit, well recommended.

The White Bear
Masham, North Yorkshire, HG4 4EN
Tel: 01765-689319.
This is not just pub food, but great food from a chalk style menu board, that changes daily in a cosy comfortable restaurant bar. It is always filled with the action of people coming and going from this popular eating establishment, and at reasonable prices. Booking is a must to avoid waiting and disappointment.

Bank Villa Guest House
Masham, Ripon, North Yorkshire, HG4 4DB
Tel: 01765 689605
Web: www.bankvilla.com
Cost: £45 Single Room. £50 Double Room. £75 Triple Room, all prices include Breakfast.
Excellent value, high standards, very comfortable and recommended.

Garden House B&B
1 Park Street Masham Ripon, North Yorkshire HG4 4HN.
Tel: 01765 689989
Email:gardenhsemasham@tiscali.co.uk
Cost: £25 - £30 per night

Venells Restaurant
7 Silver Street, Masham
Tel: 01765 689000
Web: www.vennellsrestaurant.co.uk
Email: info@vennellsrestaurant.co.uk
Opening Times:
Dinner: Tuesday – Saturday 1900 – 2130 hrs.
Lunch: Friday – Sunday 1200 – 1400hrs
Cost: Two Courses £19.95. Desserts £4.95.
Cheeses: £5.45

This is a well talked about restaurant by locals and people from far away and earned appraisals from many newspapers by producing excellent quality food. It is a must to try out to appreciate the care and dedication to provide such fine quality food..

CAFÉ & TEA ROOMS
Border House Teas. Suncatchers Café.
The Mad Hatter's Tea Room
All the above teahouses are situated fringing the Market Place of Masham, some more comfortable and expensive than the others, though all are convenient and nice.

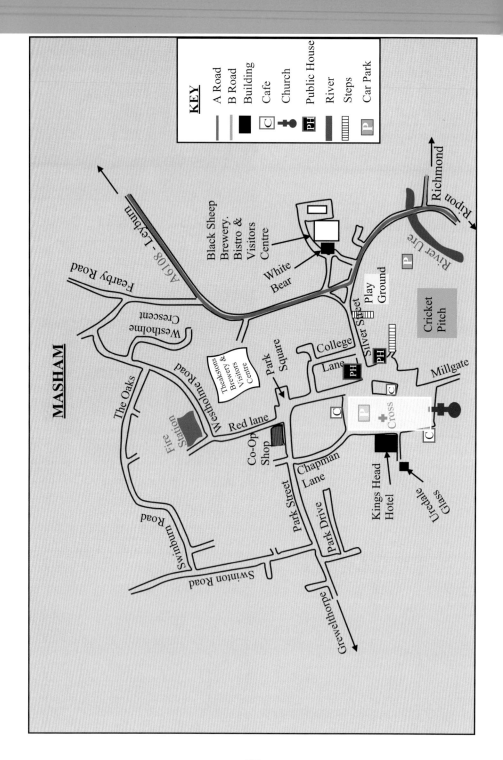

MASHAM

KEY

A Road	
B Road	
Building	
Cafe	C
Church	
Public House	PH
River	
Steps	
Car Park	P

A6108 - Leyburn

Fearby Road

Westholme Crescent

The Oaks

Westholme Road

Fire Station

Theakstons Brewery & Visitors Centre

Red lane

Co-Op Shop

Park Square

College Lane

Silver Street

Play Ground

Cricket Pitch

Black Sheep Brewery. Bistro & Visitors Centre

White Bear

River Ure

Richmond

Ripon

Swinburn Road

Swinton Road

Park Street

Park Drive

Chapman Lane

Grewelthorpe

Kings Head Hotel

Cross

Millgate

Uredale Glass

52

SECTION 4
THE RIPON ROWEL
MASHAM to DRUID'S TEMPLE

Information. This is a circular walk from Masham to Druids Temple and back to Masham using the road..
Approximate time required: 4 hours 30 minutes.
Total Distance: 16.1 km

Masham - Micklebury Lane.
(**1**) From Masham marketplace, with your back to the Church, walk along the left side passing the Kings Head Hotel and exit the marketplace via Chapman Lane.
(**2**) At the road junction turn right and walk along Park Street, crossing the road to pass the co-op shop to come to Red Lane ahead.
(**3**) Turn left down Red Lane and follow it along to the next road on the right where the fire station is at Westholme Road.
(**4**) Turn down Westholme Road and walk along passing the back of Theakstons Brewery, and eventually coming to where the road bends sharp right with a small bridge and the footpath sign on the left.
(**5**) Turn left over the small bridge and follow the road to its end passing Jameson's animal feeds factory. Here the road turns into a track, hedgerows either side. Ignore the first footpath on the left and carry straight on.

(**6**) The footpath rises to a small copse on the right, then descends to a gate next to some farm outbuildings. Here carry straight on fringing the field down to the corner where there is a gate and direction sign.
(**7**) Go through the gate on the right and turn left through a second gate, then cross the field to a stile.
(**8**) Cross the stile and turn right to fringe the field all the way, following the hedge/tree line along to a second gate.
(**9**) Go through the gate and follow the hedgerow along on the right to a stile just above Shaw's Farm.
(**10**) Cross the stile and turn right to follow the field around, up then left, fringing the field along and into the distant corner to another stile, being stone steps.
(**11**) Cross over the steps, turn right and fringe the field, and on to the road, Micklebury Lane.
Distance: 2.5 km. Approximate Time: 35 minutes

Micklebury Lane - River Burn/Bridge.

(1) Turn left and head down the lane for a short distance, to a road junction with a track leading off on the right.

(2) Turn right down what is called Low Moor Lane and follow it all the way to the end to the road junction.

Info. Looking ahead along Low Moor Lane on the right you will see the church in the village of Healey

(3) Turn left and follow the road down hill to the bridge that crosses the River Burn.

Distance: 2.2 km. Approximate Time 30 minutes.

River Burn/Bridge - Field Post.

(1) Cross the bridge over the River Burn and follow the road up to a junction.

(2) Bear right and continue up hill, passing Stonefold Farm on the left, up to a farm road to Broadmires.

(3) Turn right down Broadmires farm road, all the way to the farm and on to the gate ahead.

(4) Go through the gate and cross the field diagonally right, to a gate by the wood.

(5) Go through the gate and follow the footpath that fringes the wood on the right to the next gate at the end. The footpath/track passes through two fields ahead before meeting a gate by a wood enclosed by a wall, called Hall Wood.

(6) Go through the gate and carry on straight fringing this wood to the end with a gate.

(7) Go through this gate and follow the obvious route across the field, turning left along its course then descending down slightly to a **post** with direction signs on it that stands just before the descent into a sparse wood.

Distance: 2.2 km. Approximate Time: 29 minutes

Field Post - Druid's Temple. This is an uphill section to the road that enters Druids Wood.

(1) Turn around with your back to the post, line up the big tree on the right to the left hand tree in the distance across the field slightly up hill. Cross the field aiming for the lower tree which will guide you to a stile over this small rise to a fence crossing.

(2) At the stile look diagonally right across the fields ahead. You will see in the distant corner a gate next to a wall crossing by some steps. Walk and aim for the wall crossing.

54

(**3**) Cross the wall and follow the obvious track up hill that runs along side the wood on the left to a gate with the track cutting through the wood.

(**4**) Go through the gate and follow the footpath that cuts through the wood, where you will see on the other side Low Knowle Farm, turn right and fringe the wood on the right up to a gate supported by large stones.

(**5**) Go through this stone constructed gate and continue along the footpath that cuts straight across the field marked by a line of overhead power cables, to a stile by the road, Knowle Lane.

(**6**) Cross the stile and turn right on to the road, walk up to the wood taking the track through the gate. The track takes you straight to Druid's Temple at the centre of the wood. Distance: 1.8 km. Approximate Time: 26 minutes.

DRUID'S TEMPLE.

Druid's Temple is set in a hilltop wood close to Masham, overlooking Leighton Reservoir. It is believed to have been built in the 1820's on the instruction of William Danby of Swinton Hall, in order to provide work for the local unemployed. The pay was a shilling a day.

There is a timeless quality about this remote spot which has attracted many visitors over the years.

All sorts of images of fascination come in to ones mind when visiting this site. You just can't believe it to be built in the 1820's and for such a purpose, though, it is with curiosity that many people still come to this day for whatever their reasons.

Total Distance: 8.7 km

Druids Temple to Masham

(**1**) After exploring Druids Plantation Temple, make your way back along the track to the entrance road. Follow the road to the end where there is a road junction.

(**2**) Turn left at the road junction and follow the road down passing the farm road to Broadmires farm road which is on the left.

(**3**) Continue on following the road round and down to the road junction just above River Burn, signed Swinton.

(**4**) Follow the road around to the right at the road junction heading in the direction of Swinton.

(**5**) Follow the road on crossing a ford ahead by the footbridge and on to the next road junction with the boundary wall, which is the boundary of Swinton Park Hotel.

(**6**) Continue straight on at the boundary wall road junction. This road follows the boundary wall along on the right and eventually ending up at a road junction in front of the main entrance to the Swinton Park Hotel, and a grassed area separating the roads.

(6) Turn sharp left opposite the main hotel entrance and follow this road down and along to cross over the River Burn passing the golf course on the left. Then on over a rise down into Masham, to a road junction.

(7) Turn left at the road junction in Masham and make your way to the market square.
Distance: 7.4 km. Time: 1 hour 30 minutes.

Transport. By Car: There is plenty of parking in the market square or down by the sports pitches close to the River Ure.

On Foot: The 159 Bus Operates a service between Ripon and Masham Mondays - Saturdays at the following times:
Ripon - Masham. 0935   1140   1340 1535 1730 hrs
Masham - Ripon. 1055 1255 1455 1700 hrs

Additionally the 139 bus operates at: 1810 1830 1942 hrs Masham - Ripon.
The bus stop is located in the market place to the rear of The Boarders Cafe.

Masham Golf Course

RIPON ROWEL MAP
MASHAM - DRUID'S TEMPLE

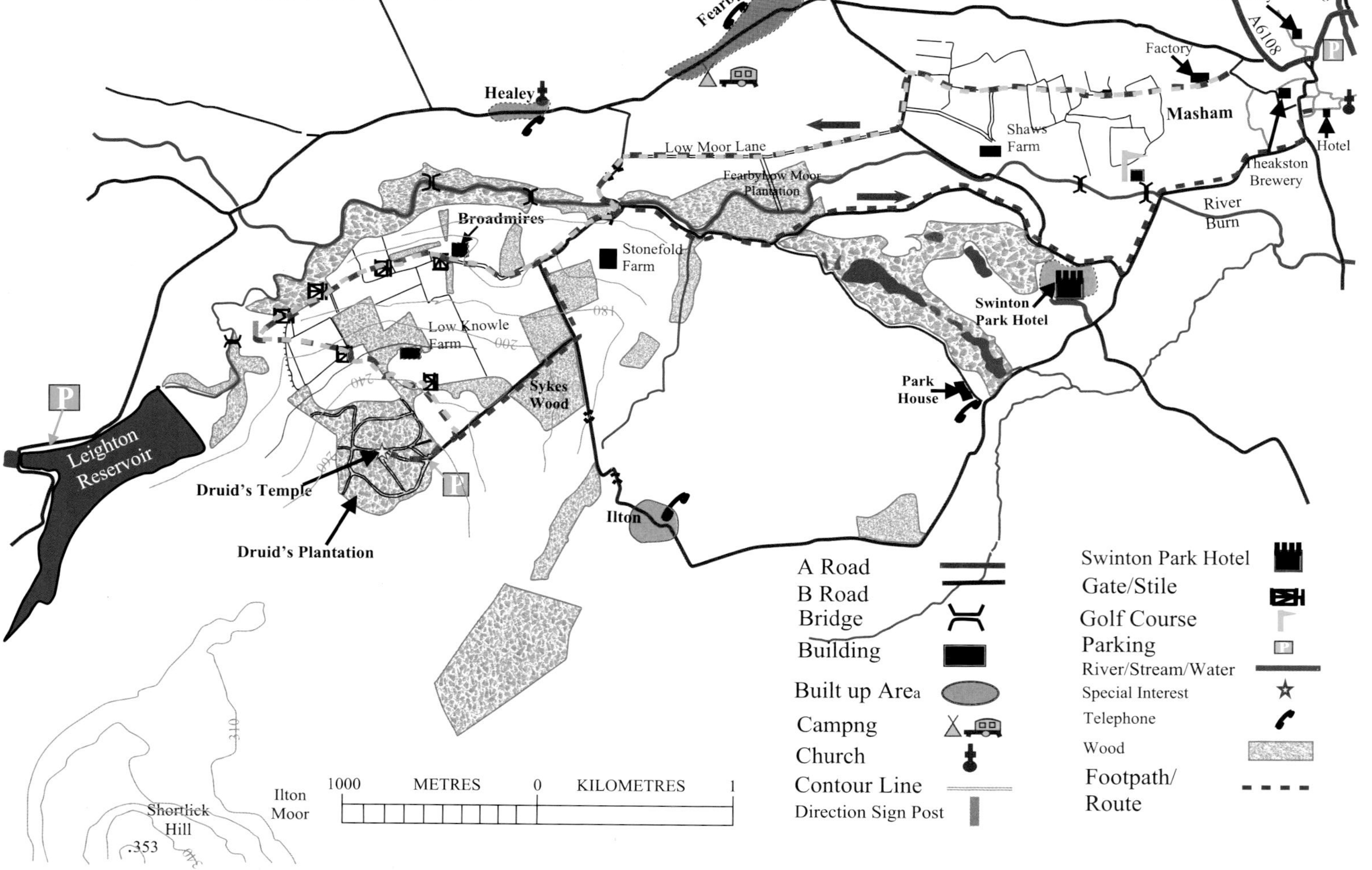
Black Sheep Brewery
ver Ure
A6108
Factory
Masham
Hotel
Theakston Brewery
River Burn
Shaws Farm
Fearby
Healey
Low Moor Lane
Fearby Low Moor Plantation
Broadmires
Stonefold Farm
Swinton Park Hotel
Low Knowle Farm
180
200
240
260
Sykes Wood
Park House
Leighton Reservoir
Druid's Temple
Druid's Plantation
Ilton
310
Shortlick Hill
.353
340
Ilton Moor
1000
METRES
0
KILOMETRES
1
A Road
B Road
Bridge
Building
Built up Area
Campng
Church
Contour Line
Direction Sign Post
Swinton Park Hotel
Gate/Stile
Golf Course
Parking
River/Stream/Water
Special Interest
Telephone
Wood
Footpath/
Route

SECTION 5
THE RIPON ROWEL
DRUIDS TEMPLE to THE DROVERS INN

Approximate time required: 2 hrs 50 minutes
Total Distance: 11.5 km

Druids Temple - Track by Black Hill House Farm.

(**1**) After visiting Druids Temple return to the road that brought you into the wood. Travel back down the road through a metal gate, that is always open, to the gate on the right with a stile crossing.

(**2**) Cross the stile and head straight passing through a second gate down to a third that opens into an open field almost level with the bottom of the farm house and a footpath direction sign..

(**3**) Go through the gate/stile and turn left as directed, here the footpath runs across the front of the farm, below it, to a stile on the right.

(**4**) Cross the stile and follow the path down hill passing through a gate on the way down to a final gate by the wood.

(**5**) Turn left through the gate and follow the track to its end, where it meets the road.

(**6**) Turn right at the road and cross over a small footbridge where it is usually a ford crossing, then follow the road up hill to the hamlet of Ilton.

(**7**) Continue along the road through Ilton to where the road bends sharp left by Manor Farm to a footpath sign and stile on the right.

(**8**) Cross the stile and head straight to the wall on the other side of this depression and boggy ground, at the wall follow it right and up into a corner to a stepping stones wall crossing.

(**9**) Cross the stepping stones over the wall and follow the wall along passing the gate opening to a wall crossing, a short distance ahead on the left.

(**10**) Go through the wall on the left and turn right heading up hill passing through the trees and bearing slightly left and up to the footpath, then up to a wall crossing.

(**11**) Go over the wall, and turn left following the only path visible, keeping on this path for a short distance to where a ruined wall crosses the path and leads up to a line of shooting butts.

(**12**) Turn right at the ruined wall and follow the path that runs along the back of the shooting butts all the way to a track by a dry stonewall and a gate.

(**13**) Turn right onto the track and head uphill for a short distance to a stile crossing over a fence.

(**14**) Cross the stile and follow the footpath that initially runs alongside a ruin of a wall on the left, that leads you to the road and a gate with a trough.
(**15**) Go over the gate, turn right and follow the road down to Black Hill House Farm, the third farm on the left.
Distance: 4.3 km. Approximate Time: 55 minutes.

Track by Black Hill House Farm - Sighting Tower by Carlesmoor Wood.

(**1**) Continue on along the road passing Hilltop Farm and Ellershaw Farm on the right, then Fir Tree Farm on the left, all the way along to a T junction before a wood.
(**2**) Turn right at the T junction signed Kirkby Malzeard, and follow the road along and around to the left then to the end of the wood continue on.
(**3**) Continue on this road over the high ground passing a road junction on the right to the wood, Newlands Wood. Continue on down to fringe Newlands Wood on the right and follow the road around to the left at the bottom, to the wall crossing on the right, opposite the old farm buildings.

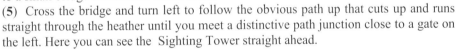

(**4**) Cross the wall and descend down the bank to a small bridge that crosses Stock Beck.
(**5**) Cross the bridge and turn left to follow the obvious path up that cuts up and runs straight through the heather until you meet a distinctive path junction close to a gate on the left. Here you can see the Sighting Tower straight ahead.
(**6**) Bear right and descend, do not go through the gate, but go down and cross Ellershaw Gill. Cross over the Gill and ascend the bank to a gate on the left.
(**7**) Go through the gate and follow the track along, which is lined left and right by dry stonewalls, all the way to the Sighting Tower. In the field prior to the tower you will see a building, this belongs to Yorkshire water and is the entrance to Carlesmoor tunnel, it contains three water tanks for water pumping.

Distance: 3.5 km. Approximate Time: 50 minutes.

SIGHTING TOWER.

This Sighting Tower was built to provide communications, and guide workers across the moors in the times of reservoir construction. It will be inline with others over distance and would have been lit and maintained by a few workers with living space provided

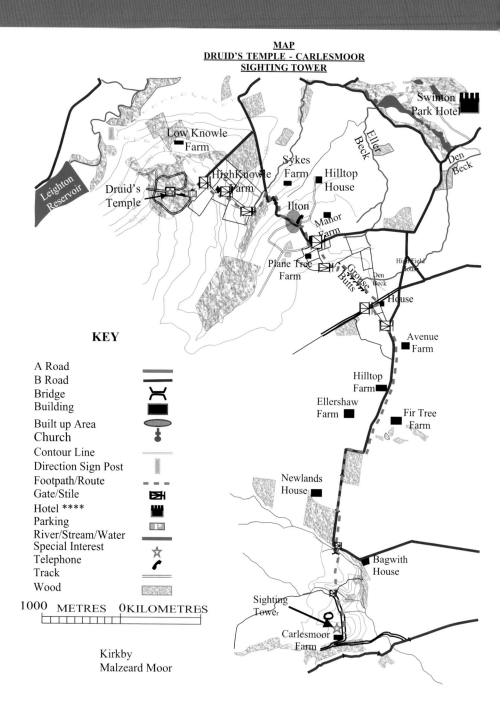

MAP
DRUID'S TEMPLE - CARLESMOOR
SIGHTING TOWER

Swinton Park Hotel

Low Knowle Farm

Eller Beck

Den Beck

Sykes Farm

Hilltop House

HighKnowle Farm

Druid's Temple

Leighton Reservoir

Ilton

Manor Farm

Plane Tree Farm

Grouse Butts

Den Beck

High Field House

House

Avenue Farm

Hilltop Farm

Ellershaw Farm

Fir Tree Farm

KEY

A Road
B Road
Bridge
Building
Built up Area
Church
Contour Line
Direction Sign Post
Footpath/Route
Gate/Stile
Hotel ****
Parking
River/Stream/Water
Special Interest
Telephone
Track
Wood

Newlands House

Bagwith House

1000 METRES 0KILOMETRES

Sighting Tower

Carlesmoor Farm

Kirkby
Malzeard Moor

close by. Today it will only be lit or used in special celebratory circumstances, like the Queen's jubilee.

Sighting Tower by Carlesmoor Wood - The Drovers Inn.

(1) Continue on the track passing the Sighting Tower on the right, and follow the track around to the right to the gate by the farm.

Information: Mobile phone coverage. Once you leave the farm area and descend there is no coverage until you are close to the Drovers Inn.

(2) Go through the gate and take the farm road that descends around to the left and runs alongside the wood on the right.

(3) Follow this track along to its end where it meets the road. Then turn left on the road and head uphill for a short distance to the signed footpath/track, on the right and a blue sign stating, "Unsuitable for Motor Vehicles".

(4) Turn right and follow the track down hill for about 500 metres crossing underneath some power lines, to a ford crossing and a little footbridge.

(5) Continue on following the track through a gate that leads you up to a track T junction with a gate on the left.

(6) Turn left through the gate and follow the track down to a footpath/track junction on the right. A direction marker points the way.

(7) Turn right and follow the footpath that leads you to a second ford crossing and a footbridge.

(8) Cross the footbridge and follow the track around to the right. The track is a gradual climb up hill straight and eventually meets the road at a bend.

(9) Join the road and head left slightly up hill to a T junction with the main road.

(10) Turn right and follow the road up to the Drovers Inn.

Distance: 3.7 km. Approximate Time: 55 minutes

Transport. To start the days walk at Druids Plantation the following taxi services are available to book, this is a perfect start to the days walk:

Ladybird Taxi. Telephone: 01765 688688. Mobile. 07843693153.
Nicholson's Mini Bus-Service: 01765 689629. Mobile. 07703349177.

The Ripon Roweller bus service operates a service that will pick you up and return you to Ripon. For details on this service please see pages 86 - 88

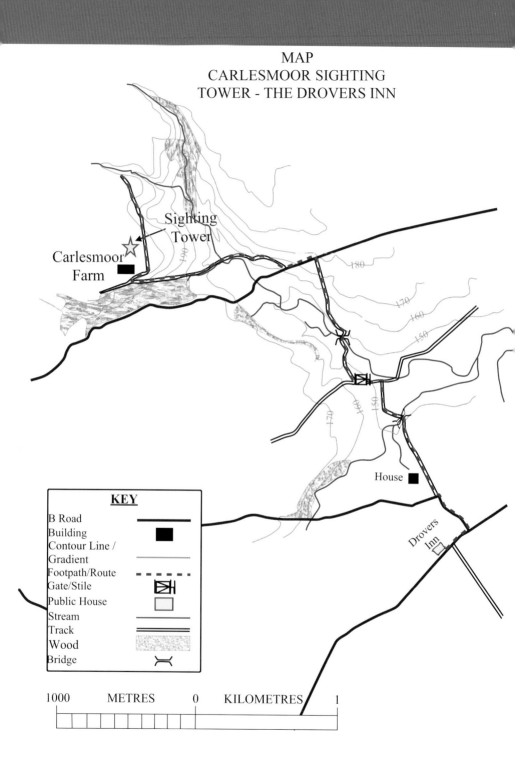

MAP
CARLESMOOR SIGHTING
TOWER - THE DROVERS INN

Sighting
Tower

Carlesmoor
Farm

House

KEY

B Road	
Building	■
Contour Line / Gradient	
Footpath/Route	- - -
Gate/Stile	
Public House	□
Stream	
Track	
Wood	
Bridge	

Drovers Inn

1000   METRES   0   KILOMETRES   1

SECTION 6
THE RIPON ROWEL
DROVERS INN - FOUNTAINS ABBEY VISITORS CENTRE

Transport: To start this day at the Drover Inn transport by taxi is the best option. The Ripon Roweller bus and the Little Red bus response services operates a transport system. For details see pages 86 - 88.

The Drovers Inn – Skelding Grange Farm.

(1) With your back to the Drovers Inn, turn left and head down the road for a very short distance, to the signed footpath track on the right hand side of the road.

(2) Turn right down the track that rises along its course, to the centre of a wood on the left. The track then descends down slightly to meet a footpath crossing, parallel to the bottom of the wood on the left.

(3) Go through the gate in front of you, the track follows a dry stonewall on the left for a short distance then cuts slightly right, diagonally over the open ground to a clump of rocks, though, the dry stonewall heads in to a corner then out to come to the same point just below the rocks.

(4) Descend with the dry stonewall on the left to Holborn Beck crossing, which is usually a wet muddy area prior to a gate; stepping stones run close to the wall to cross this area.

(5) Go through the gate and up the slope, and continue along to the track end, where it meets the road.

(6) At the road head straight and follow the road to where it bends left, you go straight on as if heading towards the farm in front of you, which is Skelding Grange Farm with two white metal gates.

Distance: 2.4 km. Time: 40 minutes

Skelding Grange – Eavestone Lake.

(1) Facing Skelding Grange Farm, by the gates, turn right along the road. The road bends right and passes: a footpath on the left, under overhead power lines and a farm on the right, before coming to a track with a metal gate on the left and a footpath sign opposite.

(2) Go through the gate on the left and follow the track downhill, through a second gate; then following a wall on the left down to a gate/stile that enters a young plantation, a little overgrown, don't go through the

gate/stile, but instead turn right and follow the wire fence along and down hill to a corner posts with a direction sign on it.

(**3**) Cross the field down and diagonally to meet a gate, close to the bottom.

(**4**) Go through the gate and follow the track down that curves left to end by a Stream and a gate on the left.

(**5**) Go through the gate and follow the footpath along the stream to a footbridge on the right.

(**6**) Cross the bridge, go over the stile in front of you and turn right, walk along to a second stile crossing,

(**7**) Head uphill following the wire fence on the left to a field corner and a stile.

(**8**) Cross the stile and turn left heading uphill, with a fence and a hedge on the left, all the way to meet a track. Here you will see a slight track that cuts right and uphill to Topham Close Farm.

(**9**) Turn left and follow this less distinguished track that cuts through the top of the fields, straight along to a gate in front of a wood.

(**10**) Go through the gate and follow the track in a curving descent to the right. Looking through the woods on your left you may catch a glimpse of Brim Brae Pond. The track descends down to the bottom of a small valley, where in front of you is a fenced in private pond.

(**11**) Turn left at the bottom and cross the small stream.

(**12**) Follow the track around to the left, and then right where it cuts through a pass in the ground, high ground left and right with low ground in the middle. The track slopes along and up passing through a gate, then gradually gaining height to a gate by a farm, where the track ends.

(**13**) Go through the gate and continue along the road straight at first then ascending and bending right, passing Eavestone Grange on the left. The road rises and then descends down passing a farm on the right, ending at the bottom of the valley with a wooded area on the left to where the road bends left.

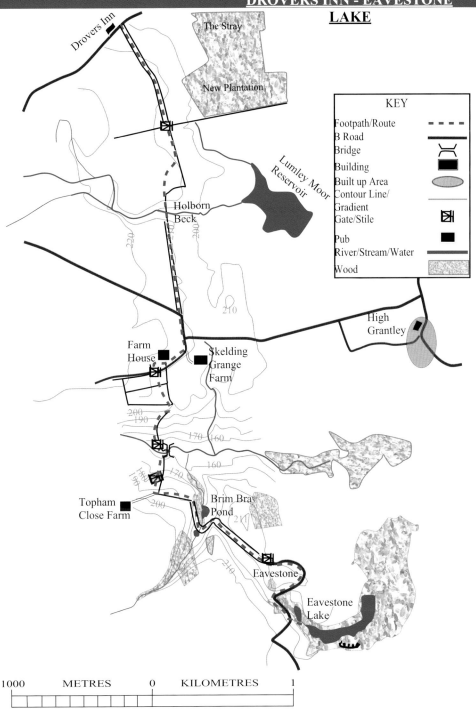

MAP
DROVERS INN - EAVESTONE
LAKE

Drovers Inn

The Stray

New Plantation

Lumley Moor Reservoir

Holborn Beck

KEY

Footpath/Route	- - - -
B Road	———
Bridge	
Building	■
Built up Area	⬭
Contour Line/ Gradient	———
Gate/Stile	✖
Pub	■
River/Stream/Water	———
Wood	

210

High Grantley

Farm House

Skelding Grange Farm

200
190

170 160

160

170

180
190

Topham Close Farm

200

Brim Bray Pond

210

240

Eavestone

Eavestone Lake

1000   METRES   0   KILOMETRES   1

(14) Follow the road around to the left and uphill for a short distance to the footpath sign that points into the wood and to Eavestone Lake.
Distance: 3.2 km. Time: 50 minutes.

EAVESTONE LAKE

This place was once described as Yorkshires little secret, and it really is, because not many of the people that live in Ripon know about it, being so close. It is a moon shaped lake sheltered in a small valley with an abundance of trees and flowers that have grown

around the sandstone rocks around its banks. Here you can walk on a windy day and be sheltered from the harsh conditions and enjoy this tranquil gem of a place, no matter what the season or weather.

Eavestone Lake - The Sawley Arms.

(1) Turn off the road and join the footpath that enters the wood.

(2) Follow the footpath along that cuts across to the far bank of Eavestone Lake. Here the footpath runs along the shore of the lake providing great views and places to sit along the route.

(3) Follow the footpath to the end of the lake and turn right where the path runs along a dam wall and over a small humpback bridge to the far side.

(4) On the far side, the footpath ascends through the wood to meet a stile overlooking a field before you.

(5) Cross the stile and cross the field left diagonally to the track by a gate.

(6) Turn left onto the track ignoring Hollin Hill Farm entrance, but continue along the track, slightly down hill, bending right, where you will end up by the front entrance of the farmhouse building.

(7) Continue on straight with the farm building on the right to a gate, pass through the gate and follow this footpath/track to its end, where it meets a field in front of you.

(8) Turn right, and fringe the field uphill for a short distance to a stile over a wall.

(9) Cross the wall and turn left to follow this wide track into a field, and then straight across to the farm ahead.

(10) Follow the track central through the farm that takes you to the B6265 Pateley Bridge/Ripon road.

(11) Turn left at the road and head down to the footpath on the right of the road, to a stile.

(12) Cross the stile and follow the path through the field to a stile in the field corner.

(13) Go over the stile and the follow the track up to cross a second stile ahead, fringing a hedgerow on the left to a footpath crossing by a concrete building on the left.

(14) Turn left, go over the stile by the building and follow the tree/hedgerow along to a field corner with a stile on the right.

(15) Turn right and cross the stile where the footpath runs alongside a field hedgerow to a stile on the left.

(16) Cross the stile and head downhill following the hedgerow on the left, eventually to a wall crossing.

(17) Go over the wall and follow the track to meet the road head. Turn right and follow the road along to the Sawley Arms.

Distance 3.5 km. Approximate Time: 55 minutes

THE SAWLEY ARMS

The village of Sawley is located a little further on passt the valley that houses Fountains Abbey, passed Spa Gill wood, southeast of High Grantley over the Pateley Bridge road. It is here that you will find the Sawley Arms, a cosy tucked away restaurant pub with traditional furnishings and layout with an open fire to greet you; providing that welcome feeling as soon as you step inside. Refreshments, lunch and dinner as well as good wines and drinks can be provided, whatever your choice, the food is always excellent, traditional English with a specials board to choose from.

The Sawley Arms can make a great day out combining Fountains Abbey with lunch providing refreshments for the Ripon Rowel walker, what better day could there be than finishing at the Sawley. Open from 1200 hrs daily.

Accommodation is available, which is cottage style. For more information and bookings: The Sawley Arms, Sawley, North Yorkshire, HG4 3QE.
Tel: 01765 620642

The Sawley Arms - Fountains Abbey Visitors Centre.

(**1**) With your back to the Sawley Arms, cross the road and head straight down the small road opposite, with a church on the right, for 15 minutes to where the footpath enters a wood, Spa Gill Wood, on the left by a stile.

(**2**) Cross the stile and follow the footpath down through the wood to cross a small humpback bridge.

(**3**) Cross the humpback bridge and turn right following the track to a gate by the edge of the wood, close to a bridge on the right.

(**4**) Go through the gate and follow the track up through the field to where it meets the road with a gate/stile.

(**5**) Cross the stile and turn left heading uphill to a track that leaves the road in a fork like action on the right.

(**6**) Leave the road and join the track on the right that cuts a corner to meet a road again at a junction.

(**7**) Cross the road and turn right, taking the footpath separated by a hedgerow, and follow this path for approximately 8 minutes to a road roundabout.

(**8**) At the roundabout turn right and walk up to Fountains Abbey Visitors Centre.

Distance: 2.9 km. Approximate Time: 40 minutes

Total Distance: 12 km. Total Time: 3 hours 15 minutes

Transport: The Ripon Roweller stops opposite the main entrance of the visitors centre, providing transport to Ripon Monday - Saturday on the following times: 1417 and 1517 hrs

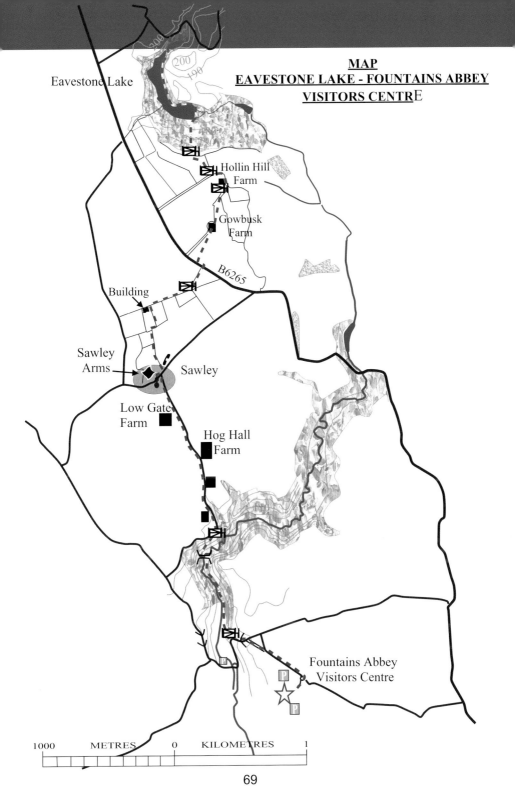

MAP
EAVESTONE LAKE - FOUNTAINS ABBEY
VISITORS CENTRE

Eavestone Lake

Hollin Hill
Farm

Gowbusk
Farm

B6265

Building

Sawley
Arms

Sawley

Low Gate
Farm

Hog Hall
Farm

Fountains Abbey
Visitors Centre

1000   METRES   0   KILOMETRES   1

SECTION 7
THE RIPON ROWEL
FOUNTAINS ABBEY VISITORS CENTRE – RED LION/ SOUTH STAINLEY

Transport: To start the day the Ripon Roweller 139 Bus is the best way to get to the Visitors Centre. Bus Times from Ripon bus station are as follows: 1030 or 1320 hrs

FOUNTAINS ABBEY VISITORS CENTRE

This is a series of ground level buildings only, where the architecture catches your eye with the use of wooden beams and the curved shaped roof that can be seen and enjoyed both inside and out, making the centre a natural surround to the wooded area it fringes. The buildings have been built joined to form a circular shape, consisting of offices, toilets, the National Trust shop and Abbey entrance, and opposite, the café/restaurant that presents a clean open area to sit offering a wide range of choice by self service, snacks and meals at very reasonable prices. The middle of the centre, outside, provides a sheltered by the buildings, and there is ample parking facilities to meet the needs of the many visitors. A good place to start and finish your visit to Fountains Abbey.

FOUNTAINS ABBEY & STUDLEY ROYAL DEER PARK

In 1699 John Aislabie inherited the estate and in 1718 he became Chancellor of the Exchequer. After a disaster in his career he returned to North Yorkshire and commenced to transform the valley and the course of the River Skell, by forming a series of still water gardens and features along its route. Beautiful turfed lawns were formed and used to separate the water features. Paths and tracks cross the whole area and a variety of trees were used to enrich the valley in vegetation. Trees such as Pines, Elms, Beech and Yew were used along the course of the valley.

In the 1730s the construction of the garden buildings and structures began; The Banqueting House, Grotto, Octagon Tower, Rustic bridge, Serpentine tunnel,

and the Temples. John Aislabie died in 1742, his son William Aislabie continued his fathers work and sealed the entire garden with the purchase of the Abbey and Fountains Hall.

The Deer Park covers 400 acres and was already established at the time of John Aislabie inheritance, he enhanced the Parks natural beauty with the introduction of a variety of trees, scattered and interspersed throughout, and along the remarkable avenue, that falls in line with Ripon Cathedral. The

trees here are mainly Beech, Oak, Sweet Chestnut and Horse Chestnut. The other ground feature in the park is the small valley that continues along the banks of the River Skell, known has the Valley of the Seven Bridges, because of the little humpback bridges along its course. Today nothing has changed except the ownership, which is now owned by the National Trust. There are several buildings and structures of distinction in the park:

The Obelisk, by St Mary's Gate which was erected in 1805 to take the place of a funerary pyramid, placed by William Aislabie as a memorial to his father in 1742.

St Mary's Church. Was built by the architect William Burges for the first Marquess and Marchioness of Ripon in the 19th Century. Its design together with the use of materials meant that no expense was spared, to elaborate a strong belief in Christianity. It is only open certain times of the year.

Studley Royal House, Stable Block Building. Studley Royal House was originally known as Tudor Manor, inherited by John Aislabie, severely damaged by fire in 1716, then rebuilt only to be completely destroyed by fire in 1946. The prominent square shaped building standing today was the stable building to the house, which is now privately owned.

Fountains Abbey Visitors Centre – St Mary's Church in Studley Royal Deer Park.

(1) With your back to the Visitors Centre make your way to the road, and join the footpath on the right just before the roundabout.

(2) Follow the footpath down to the roundabout on your left and continue along screened from the road by shrubs and trees all the way to a gate on the right that enters Studley Deer Park.

(3) Turn right and proceed through the gate and follow the park road for a very short distance to St Mary's Church on the left.

Distance: 700 metres. Approximate Time: 10 minutes.

St Mary's Church – Studley Perimeter Gate.

(1) Walk down the park road passing St Mary's Church to the second road junction on the right.

(2) Turn right and head downhill to the Park lake and take the left hand track.

(3) Follow the path around that fringes the lake to a footbridge crossing over to the far side, close to the wooded area.

(4) Turn left and follow the footpath along this small valley, known as the Valley of the Seven Bridges, crossing a number of small humpback bridges to the perimeter park wall and a gate/stile. Distance: 1.8km. Approximate Time: 22 minutes

Studley Perimeter Gate/Stile – Bench at Road/Track Junction.

(1) Go through the Gate/Stile and follow the footpath along through the bottom of this valley to a footbridge on the right.

(2) Cross the footbridge, turn left and then right heading uphill to a path crossroads at the top.

(3) Turn sharp left where the footpath leads you to a Gate/Stile entering a field.

(4) Go through the Gate/Stile and follow the footpath slightly left and up, then following a line of trees along and down hill to another Gate/Stile at the road.

(5) Go through the Gate/Stile and turn right heading uphill to a road track junction on the left and a bench set back.

Distance: 1.5 km. Approximate Time: 22 minutes.

Bench at Road/Track Junction – Markenfield Hall.

(1) Continue on along the road passing the track on the right, to descend down to a cattle grid crossing at Bland Close Farm.

(2) Cross the cattle grid and head straight using the hedgerow to follow on the right to a stile crossing.

(3) Cross the stile and follow the footpath to the next field boundary with a wood on the right and power lines crossing through the field. Head straight and follow the wood along to where the power cables cut through the wood. Here is a wall stile crossing.

(4) Cross the wall and follow the path for a short distance to a stile overlooking a large field with Markenfield Hall at the far end of the field.

(5) Cross the stile and head for the left side of the hall crossing the field to a wooden fence that runs the length of the Hall.

(6) Continue on in the same direction, following the wooden fence along and then to a wall crossing by some steps, level with the Hall Gatehouse.
Distance: 1.2 km Approximate Time: 16 minutes

MARKENFIELD HALL

Markenfield Hall is just 3 miles south of Ripon just off the A61, the Ripon to Harrogate road. It is a Mediaeval house that has its own mediaeval Chapel, surrounded by a moat occupied by black swans. It is full of history, being built in the fourteenth century by Sir John Markenfield and is, still, to this day in the hands of his descendants, being a private home. It is a quiet place that is approached through farm buildings, and you get an enchanted feeling once the gatehouse and moat come into view. Today Markenfield Hall is open to the public: 1 – 14 May and 18 June – 1 July. 1400 – 1700 hrs daily. Also weddings can be arranged here. Tel: 01765 692303

Markenfield Hall – Road/Track Junction at Thwaite Lane.

(1) Cross the wall and head straight to the entrance of Markenfield Hall and turn left passing the farm buildings left and right of you, to the farm road.

(2) Turn right onto the farm road and go up to a gate on the left that enters a field.

(3) Head straight through this field following the slight track cut in the ground to the second field by a broken down wall and a footpath sign.

(4) Pass into the second field and follow the fence along on the left of you to a Gate/Stile ahead.

(5) Go through the Gate/Stile and follow this track along to where it overlooks a field directly in front of you.

(6) The footpath crosses this field slightly right to the right edge of the trees on the far side leading to a gate.

(7) Go through the Gate/Stile and turn left heading down a bridleway and track that meets the road ahead.
Distance: 1.2km. Approximate Time: 15 minutes.

73

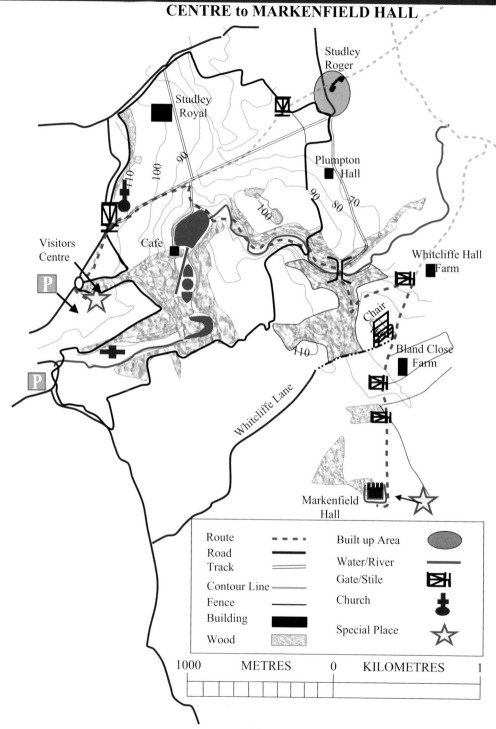

Road/Track Junction at Thwaite Lane – Waterloo Farm Road Footpath Junction.

(**1**) At the road turn right, then right again, heading uphill slightly marked by cul-de-sac signs left and right of the road, to a track junction by a direction sign. 250 metres, approximately 2 minutes 45 seconds.

(**2**) Follow the road around to the left passing a gate into a field on the left prior to a wood.

(**3**) Continue along slowly following a hedgerow on the left to just before the first house on the right. Here the footpath sign is a little hidden, but there is a break in the hedgerow on the left, where the footpath starts and leaves the road. Note if you are level with the house on the right, then you have gone past the footpath.

(**4**) Turn left off the road taking the footpath through the wood along and then downhill to Waterloo Farm and the road footpath junction.

Total Distance this leg: 900 metres. Time: 10 minutes.

Waterloo Farm Road Footpath Junction – Markington Main Road.

(**1**) At the junction with the road turn right and walk towards a metal gate that enters a field.

(**2**) Go through the gate and head straight following the edge along on the right, to the end of the field, then left to a gate stile.

(**3**) Cross the stile and follow the hedgerow along on the right, with power lines above, the path curves to the left and descends down to meet some sports pitches.

(**4**) At the sports pitches follow the footpath around the field close to the pavilion. Then go through a gap in the hedgerow and border the cricket pitch passing the pavilion on the right to a tree by a Gate/Stile.

(**5**) Go through the Gate/Stile, pass a cottage on the left to the road. Turn left, downhill to the Main Road in Markington.

Distance: 1.1 km. Approximate Time: 14 minutes.

MARKINGTON.

This is a small quiet linear village not far from the A61, Ripon – Harrogate Road. It has all the normal facilities of a small village with a Post Office shop at one end, schools and two pubs along its main street, with the cricket pitch at the south end.

Accommodation

The Hob Green Hotel & Restaurant. This lovely warm and cosy hotel that is set just outside Markington has plenty of charm and character. You walk in, and straight away you feel at home among the comfortable layout and furnishings. This together with the helpful and attentive staff make the Hob Green the perfect match to compliment any occasion, which is set in 800 acres close to Fountains Abbey. Highly recommend given the functionality and quality that this hotel provides.

Restaurant. The restaurant is located on the ground floor with views looking across to the award winning gardens. The menu, which changes daily offers a wide range of traditional English food, with a full range of mouth watering choices per course, makes this restaurant the place to come for a special treat. You could not want for a better place to eat and enjoy a meal.

Tariff: Accommodation range, starts at £93 to £185 B&B, single room to a suite.

> Breakfast, from £10
> Sunday Lunch, from £18.95.
> Table D'Hote, from £12.95
> Table D'Hote Dinner, from £26.50

Contact:Tel. 01423 770031.
Web: www.hobgreen.com.
Email: info@hobgreen.com

Pubs & Inns

The Yorkshire Hussar Inn This is a 16th Century building with stone flagged floors. It has been a pub since 1850. Today it has plenty of character and is very much a community asset. Live music nights are a regular event and it is a relief if you find it open for refreshments along the Ripon Rowel walk. This is a family run pub, though, you will probably only find the pub open in the evenings. Tel: 01765 677715.

The Cross Keys. Run by the same family as the Yorkshire Hussar. Tel: 01765 677555.

Markington Main Road – A61 Track Road Junction.
(1) At Markington main road go straight across and uphill slightly, bear left onto a track.
(2) Follow the track along and down slightly to a track bend, passing a footpath on the left, and on eventually coming level with a pond in the field on the left.
(3) Continue along the track that eventually comes to a sharp bend left in front of a metal gate with a footpath direction sign.
(4) Go through the gate and fringe the field, following the hedge on the right over a small rise and down to the field corner to a bridge that crosses a stream.
(5) Cross the bridge, turn left then follow the path that leads up slightly and along, all the way to the A61 main Ripon to Harrogate road.
Distance: 2.2 km. Approximate Time: 28 minutes

A61 Track Road Junction – Red Lion Pub/ South Stainley.

(1) Turn right and use the grass verge to walk along the fringe of this busy road to firm ground by the bus stop.
(2) This is the place to catch the Number 36 bus back into Ripon. Cross the road and you are at the Red Lion that serves basic food and hot and cold drinks.
Distance: 350 metres. Approximate Time: 5 minutes

Total Distance: 10.95 km. Total Time: 2 hours 24 minutes, without breaks

Bus Timetable – Red Lion South Stainley to Ripon: Monday - Friday
1045 1105 1125 1145 1205 1225 1245 1305 1325 1345 1405 1425 1445 1505 1525 1545
1605 1625 1645 1715 1735 1755 up to 2320 hrs.

Saturdays
1105 then at these times past each hour: 25, 45, 05
Sundays
1150 1220 1250 1320 1350 1420 1450 1520 1550 1620
1720 1820 1920 2020 2120 2220 2320 hrs

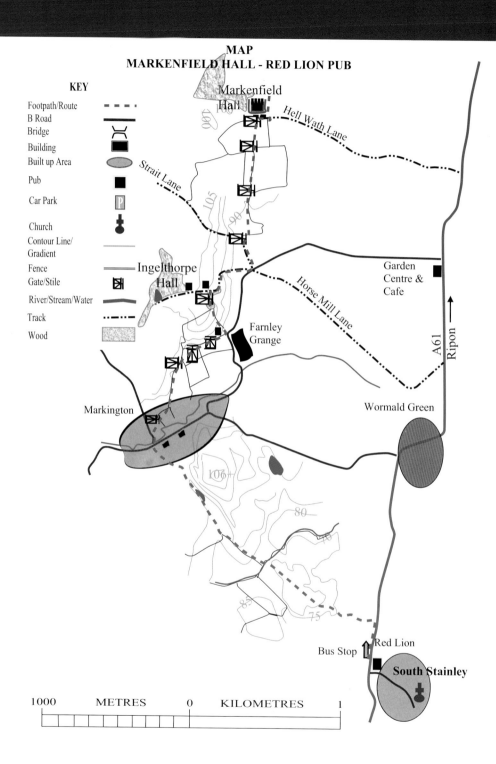

MAP
MARKENFIELD HALL - RED LION PUB

KEY

Footpath/Route	
B Road	
Bridge	
Building	
Built up Area	
Pub	
Car Park	P
Church	
Contour Line/ Gradient	
Fence	
Gate/Stile	
River/Stream/Water	
Track	
Wood	

Markenfield Hall

Hell Wath Lane

Strait Lane

Ingelthorpe Hall

Garden Centre & Cafe

Horse Mill Lane

A61

Ripon

Farnley Grange

Markington

Wormald Green

106

80

75

85

Bus Stop

Red Lion

South Stainley

1000   METRES   0   KILOMETRES   1

SECTION 8
THE RIPON ROWEL
RED LION - RIPON CATHEDRAL

Information. An ideal start time for this section would be to take the 1005 hrs No 36 Bus from Ripon bus station to the Red Lion PH South Stainley. This will allow you to take advantage of refreshments in either the Hare & Hounds, Burton Leonard or the Lamb & Flag pub in Bishop Monkton.

SOUTH STAINLEY

South Stainley is located adjacent to the A61, Ripon – Harrogate road, 2.5 miles N.E of Ripley and 6 miles S.E of Ripon, marked by the Red Lion public house. The village consists of farms and houses along its course with Stainley Beck cutting through. At the end of the village road is the Parish church of St Wilfrid, that stands out once you arrive at its doorstep. A picturesque church that displays stocks in its entrance.

Red Lion Pub South Stainley - Burton Leonard

(**1**) At the road junction with the A61/ Red Lion Pub, turn left down Church Lane and follow the road through South Stainley, over the bridge that displays a water pump on the right, up to the church on the left.

Distance 500 metres, approximate time: 6 minutes

(**2**) Continue on passing the church and follow the track along to a second bridge, just below Stainley Hall on the left.

(**3**) Cross the bridge and continue along eventually ascending, passing a track on the right and a wood on the left, to gain the high ground, then on, to come to a track junction ahead.

Distance: Serial 2 & 3, 1.5 kilometres. Approximate Time: 20 minutes

(**4**) Turn left at the track junction and follow the track along, passing a track on the right and then along descending down to a track junction above Limekiln farm.

Distance: 800 metres. Approximate Time: 12 minutes

(**5**) Turn left at the track junction and head direct towards the buildings in front, cross the stream by the footbridge below the farm buildings and cross the stile to join the farm road.

(**6**) Follow this road left passing in between the buildings and up. The road passes the wood on the right and ascends, then eventually levels off at the top of the hill. Continue on along to meet a road junction ahead separated by a seat and a

footpath direction sign. Distance: Serials 5&6, 1 km. Approximate Time: 18 minutes.

(7) Turn left at the bench with the road junction and follow the road up passing the houses on the left to the main road in the village of Burton Leonard. Turn right and follow the road down to the Post Office. Distance: 700 metres. Approximate Time: 10 minutes.

BURTON LEONARD

Burton Leonard is located 4 miles N.E of Ripley and 5 miles S of Ripon not far from the A61 main Harrogate to Ripon Road. The features of this village catch your eye as the road sweeps through passing three separate greens along the course of the village. Here you will find large trees providing seating and shelter at their bases for the tired traveller, or just nice places to rest. The village is very picturesque with its houses and layout together with St Leonards church  prominent in the centre; built about 1870, the church has a clean appearance about it and inside the stained glass windows are a work of art and of beauty.

Pubs & Restaraunts

The Hare & Hounds. Tel:01765 677355. This is a great stop at any time of the day, open from 1130 hrs for tea and coffee, with lunch served from 1200 hrs. This is a full restaurant pub that provides a wide variety of choices with three courses available, and a wine list with wines from around the world.

Good value for money whatever your choice or reason to stop. Well recommended

Burton Leonard - Bishop Monkton.

(1) Continue on past the Post office on the right and the church on the left, to the first road on the left that runs alongside the church. Turn left and follow this road passing all the houses on the right, out of the village completely to a road junction just before a house on the left. Distance: 500 metres. Approximate Time: 6 minutes.

(2) Turn left and follow the road to its end, it turns into a track and turns left and right to go straight on to a gate/stile in front of a field.

(3) Go through the gate and pass to the left the pylon stands, aiming for wooden pylon in front of you and downhill. In the middle of the hedgerow ahead you will see a stile.

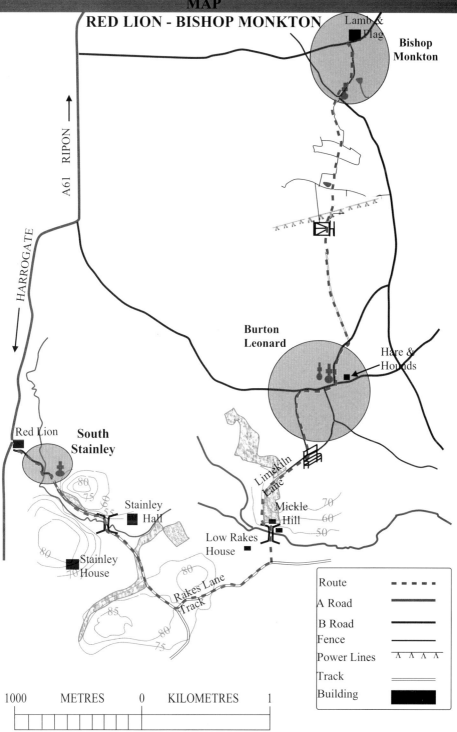

MAP
RED LION - BISHOP MONKTON

(4) Cross the stile and head straight ahead to a hedgerow corner and a stile crossing. The footpath follows a hedgerow along on the right to cross two other stiles ahead, either side of a field.

(5) Follow the path slightly left to meet a track that cuts through a camping site, then on to the road junction in Bishop Monkton, opposite a church. Distance: 1.9 km. Approximate Time: 27 minutes for serials 2,3&4.

(6) At the road go straight across passing the church on the right. Follow this road along bending to the left then head straight to a road junction ahead, to the Lamb & Flag public house on the other side of the road.

Distance: 500 metres. Approximate Time: 6 minutes.

BISHOP MONKTON

Bishop Monkton is located 4 miles South of Ripon and 4 miles from Boroughbridge. The village features St John the Baptist Church, built in 1879 with a spire that can be seen from miles around. Leading off next to the church is a stream that runs down and through the village, with green lawns to one side, and small bridgeways to step across to access the many different picturesque stone houses along its route. There are two working farms in the village, Ivy House, and The Limes

Pubs & Restaraunts

The Lamb & Flag, this a traditional free house pub that is very much a community style pub serving food and refreshments at key times. The food is excellent, chosen from a chalkboard menu displayed around and on the pub walls, at reasonable prices.

This is an excellent place to eat, and a great place to stop on this walk for lunch or refreshments.

Bishop Monkton - Ripon Cathedral

(1) Out of the pub, cross the road and back up the road you came down to a track on the left, just opposite the beginning of the building of the Masons Arms Distance: 200 metres. Approximate Time: 3 minutes.

(2) Turn left and head down the track straight, passing a track on the left, to where the track eventually turns sharp right. Here ignore this right turn, and head straight on.

(**3**) Continue on straight, the track descends down and narrows into a footpath to the 90 deg bend left. Distance: 1.3 km. Approximate Time: 18 minutes.

(**4**) Follow the footpath around the bend, then on along this narrow path, passing through a gate then over a stile to follow a hedgerow along on the left to its end. Then cross the field to a metal gate.
Distance: 600 metres. Approximate Time: 10 minutes.

Alternative Wet Weather Route. In wet weather or when the river is in flood, this alternate route will save your feet from getting extremely wet and muddy.

In Bishop Monkton with your back to the Lamb & Flag turn left and follow the road along and eventually out of Bishop Monkton, too Just before the sign Bishop Monkton, you will see a footpath sign and a gate on the left.
Distance: 1.2 km. Time: 15 minutes.

(**5**) Turn left at the road and walk along to the signed footpath and gate/stile on the right. This is just after the Village Sign, Bishop Monkton. Distance: 200 metres. Approximate Time: 2 minutes.

(**6**) Turn right go through the gate then through a second gate to follow the footpath along straight at first, then in a wide curve to the River Ure, in front of you. Distance: 650 metres. Approximate Time: 8 minutes.

(**7**) Turn left at the river and follow the river up stream to the locks at Ripon Canal. Distance: 1 km. Approximate Time: 13 minutes.

(**8**) Cross the locks and follow the footpath along that runs beside the canal, passing two humpback bridges, a marina on the left then a second on the right next to the second set of locks. Continue along to the third set of locks close to the main road ahead.
Distance: 2.6 km. Approximate Time:34 minutes.

(**9**) Pass the locks on the left to where the canal bears left. Continue on following the canal almost to its end, to where there is a gap on the right between the houses. Distance: 1 km. Approximate Time: 12 minutes.

(**10**) Turn right in to the gap between the houses and the wall. Cross the road and head down to the Water Rat Pub, and over the footbridge ahead. Cross the bridge and follow the road up to the first turning on the

left, below the Cathedral wall; this road runs alongside the bottom of the Cathedral graveyard.

(11) Turn left and walk down this road passing a house on the left with round windows and passing Cathedral Hall on the right to a pathway that heads up some steps through an archway to the Cathedral.

Distance: 600 metres. Approximate Time: 7 minutes.

Total Distance: 15.55 km. Total Approximate Time (excluding breaks: 3 hours 33.5 minutes

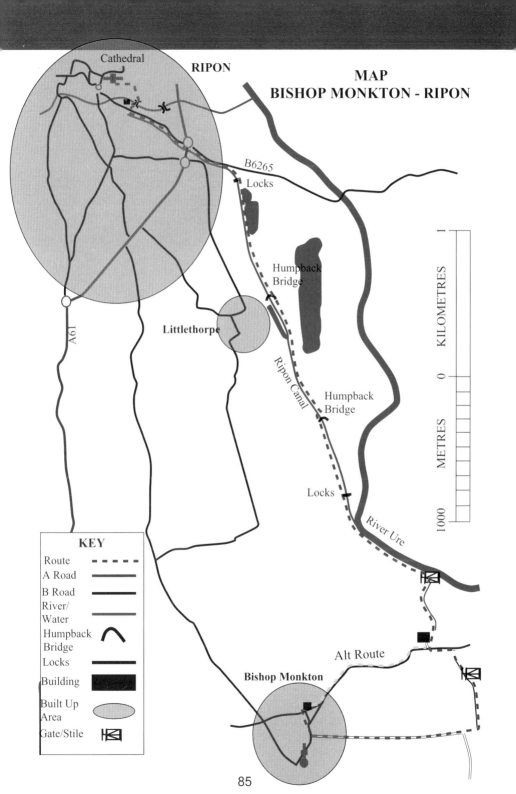

MAP
BISHOP MONKTON - RIPON

Cathedral

RIPON

B6265

Locks

Humpback
Bridge

Littlethorpe

Ripon Canal

Humpback
Bridge

A61

Locks

River Ure

Alt Route

Bishop Monkton

KILOMETRES

METRES

1

0

1000

KEY

Route	- - - -
A Road	———
B Road	———
River/ Water	———
Humpback Bridge	⌒
Locks	—
Building	■
Built Up Area	⬭
Gate/Stile	⌗

TRANSPORT

There are a number of bus services that operate around the Ripon Rowel. The services are as follows:

159 Ripon - Masham Monday - Saturday.

Ripon	0935 - 1140 - 1340 - 1535 - 1730 hrs
North Stainley	0945 - 1150 - 1350 - 1545 - 1741 hrs
West Tanfield	0949 - 1154 - 1354 - 1549 - 1745 hrs
Masham	1003 - 1203 - 1403 - 1603 - 1803 hrs

159 Masham - Ripon Monday - Saturday

Masham	0855 - 1055 - 1255 - 1455 - 1700 hrs
West Tanfield	0909 - 1109 - 1307 - 1509 - 1712 hrs
North Stainley	0912 - 1112 - 1310 - 1512 - 1715 hrs
Ripon	0922 - 1122 - 1320 - 1522 - 1725 hrs

138 Ripon Roweller Monday - Saturday

Ripon	0555 - 0655 - 1740 - 1800 - 1900 hrs
Galphay	0607 - 0707 - 1752 - 1812 - 1912 hrs
Kirkby Malzeard	0612 - 0712 - 1757 - 1817 - 1917 hrs
Grewelthorpe	0617 - 0717 - 1802 - 1822 - 1922 hrs
Masham	0625 - 0725 - 1810 - 1830 - 1930 hrs

139 Ripon Roweller Ripon/ Fountains Abbey & Villages. Monday - Saturday

Ripon Bus Station	1030	Ripon Bus Station	1320 - 1535
Deer Park	1041	Markington	1320
Studley Roger	1046	Sawley	1341
Fountains Visitors Centre	1053	Grantley	1346
Aldfield	1053	Winksley	1354
Galphay	1108	Galphay	1359
Winksley	1113	Aldfield	1414
Grantley	1121	Fountains Visitors Centre	1417 - 1547
Sawley	1126	Studley Roger	1421
Markington	1137	Deer Park	1426
Ripon Bus Station	1147	Ripon Bus Stion	1437 - 1559

Ripon Rowller Response Service. The Ripon Roweller bus operates a response service for wherever and whenever you want to travel around the Ripon area. To use this service you must register by filling in the application form overleaf, which will enable you to use the service throughout the year. Bookings Telephone 01423 526655

Ripon Roweller Registration Form

wQad0023f

Little Red Bus – is part of an Independent Voluntary Organisation which aims to provide opportunities to use affordable accessible transport to anyone in the Harrogate District especially those who have difficulty in using other public transport. This service enables people to retain their independence and lead full and active lives.

Name...

Reg. User No...............(Office use only)

Address..

Telephone No's...... **Post Code**.............. **Concessionary Pass No**...................

Age: under 16..... **16/25**..... **25/50**..... **50/65**..... **over 65**.........

If you are living where there is limited transport or no public transport, please state what is available..

If door to door service : Type of accommodation and if easily accessible..

Do you use any of the following? please circle the following

Wheel Chair.......... **Walking Frame/Stick**.............**Other**.....................

Do you wish to provide an escort Yes/ No

How did you hear about Little Red Bus? Friend_____ **Relative**_____ **Press**_____

Doctor/Hospital/Clinic_____**Social Worker/Day Care**____**School/College**_____

Voluntary organisation_____**Other**_____

If you would like to help or support this project – donations can be sent to HDCT

LITTLE RED BUS
Unit 4, Saltergate Business Park, Burley Bank Road, Killinghall, North Yorkshire, HG3 2BX
tel: 01423 526655 • fax: 01423 528219
email: info@littleredbus.co.uk • web: www.littleredbus.co.uk

Reg No. 25530 R. Harrogate District Community Transport Ltd

87

Return Address. Little Red Bus, Unit 4, Saltergate Buisness Park, Burley Bank Road, Killinghall, North Yorkshire, HG3 2BX.
Tel: 01423 526655.
Email: info@littleredbus.co.uk
Web: www.littleredbus.co.uk

36 Ripon - Harrogate

Monday - Fridays

Ripon - Red Lion
0755 - 0820 - 0840 - 0925 - 0945 - 1005 - 1025 - 1045 -then ever 20 minutes

Red Lion PH - Ripon
0745 - 0815 - 0840 - 0905 - 0945 - 1005 - 1025 - 1045 - 1105 - 1125 - 1145 - 1205 - 1225 - 1245 - 1305 - 1325 - 1345 - 1405 - 1425 - 1445 - 1505 - 1525 - 1545 - 1605. Then every 20 minutes

Saturdays

Ripon - Red Lion
0745 - 0805 - 0825 - 0845 - 0905 - 0945. Then at these minutes past the hour: 05 - 25 - 45

Red Lion - Ripon
0745 - 0805 - 0825 - 0845 - 0925 - 0945 - 1005 - 1025 - 1045 - 1105. Then at these minutes past the hour:
25 - 45 - 05

Sundays

Ripon - Red Lion
0945 - 1015 - 1045 - 1115 - 1145 - 1215 - 1245 - 1315. Then every at these minutes past the hour:
15 - 45.

Red Lion - Ripon
0950 - 1020 - 1050 - 1120 - 1150 - 1220 - 1250 - 1320. Then at these minutes past the hour:
50 - 20 up to 1820 then 60 minutes there after.

Taxi

Bob Peacock's Taxi Service Tel: 07742716505
Lady bird   07843693153 Land Line 01765 688688
Nicholson's   07703349177 Land Line 01765 689629

Note:
1. All times are accurate at the time of going to press.
2. Those intending to use the Ripon Roweller/Little Red Bus services are directed to confirm bus timings by telephone, or by visiting the web site stated above.